ONE FOR THE AGES

The 2004-05 Fighting Illini's March to the Arch

The News-Gazette

SPORTS PUBLISHING L.L.C.

www.SportsPublishingLLC.com

The News-Gazette

EDITOR AND PUBLISHER: John Foreman
EXECUTIVE EDITOR: John Beck
MANAGING EDITOR: Dan Corkery
SPORTS EDITOR: Jim Rossow
PHOTO EDITOR: Darrell Hoemann

SP Sports Publishing L.L.C.
www.SportsPublishingLLC.com

PUBLISHERS: Peter L. Bannon and Joseph J. Bannon Sr.
SENIOR MANAGING EDITOR: Susan M. Moyer
ACQUISITIONS EDITOR: Joseph J. Bannon Jr.
DEVELOPMENTAL EDITOR: Doug Hoepker
ART DIRECTOR: K. Jeffrey Higgerson
DUST JACKET DESIGN: Joseph T. Brumleve and Dustin Hubbart
BOOK LAYOUT: Jim Henehan
IMAGING: Dustin Hubbart
VICE PRESIDENT OF SALES AND MARKETING: Kevin King
MEDIA AND PROMOTIONS MANAGERS: Nick Obradovich (regional), Randy Fouts (national), Maurey Williamson (print)

Front and back cover photos: Jonathan Daniel/Getty Images

Hard cover ISBN: 1-59670-132-3
Soft cover ISBN: 1-59670-134-x

© 2005 by *The News-Gazette*

All rights reserved. Except for use in a review, the reproduction or utilization of this work in any form or by any electronic, mechanical, or other means, now known or hereafter invented, including xerography, photocopying, and recording, and in any information storage and retrieval system, is forbidden without the written permission of the publisher.

Printed in the United States

Sports Publishing L.L.C.
804 North Neil Street
Champaign, IL 61820

Phone: 1-877-424-2665
Fax: 217-363-2073
Web site: www.SportsPublishingLLC.com

Contents

Editor's Note 4
Preseason 6

Regular Season
Game 4: Gonzaga (11/27/04) 8
Game 5: Wake Forest (12/1/04) 12
Beyond X's and O's: Roger Powell 18
Game 11: Missouri (12/22/04) 24
Game 14: Cincinnati (12/31/04) 28
Beyond X's and O's: Luther Head, Dee Brown and Deron Williams 32
Game 19: Iowa (1/20/05) 36
Game 20: Wisconsin (1/25/05) 40
Game 21: Minnesota (1/29/05) 46
Beyond X's and O's: Centennial Celebration 50
Game 22: Michigan State (2/1/05) 52
Beyond X's and O's: Bruce Weber 58
Game 29: Purdue (3/3/05) 62
Game 30: Ohio State (3/6/05) 68

Big Ten Tournament
Quarterfinals: Northwestern (3/11/05) 72
Semifinals: Minnesota (3/12/05) 74
Championship: Wisconsin (3/13/05) 80

NCAA Tournament
Round 1: Fairleigh Dickinson (3/17/05) 84
Round 2: Nevada (3/19/05) 88
Sweet Sixteen: Wisconsin-Milwaukee (3/24/05) 92
Elite Eight: Arizona (3/26/05) 96
Final Four: Louisville (4/2/05) 106
Championship: North Carolina (4/4/05) 112

Season Statistics 122
Season Results 123

Editor's Note

Why analyze magic?

You can watch the illusionist's hands, study each feint and diagram each flourish. You'll still never quite comprehend everything that's happened right before your very eyes. The whole is simply something greater than the sum of the parts. In the end, it's more pleasant to assume that pixie dust really works.

The same might be said of the 2004-05 Fighting Illini. There's no singular reason why they were quite so capable on the court. The whole was simply greater than the parts. Call it chemistry—or magic. But there's no discounting either their success or the allure they held for their fans across the Great Orange Nation.

You and I saw it coming all along, long before it was "discovered" by the so-called experts, long before the Diggers and the Dickie V's ever begrudgingly climbed aboard our bright orange bandwagon. By the time Bruce Weber drove his first-year team deep into 2004's March Madness, the believers already had begun anticipating what was ahead. They watched in nervous expectation to see their opinion validated at the expense of Gonzaga, Cincinnati and the others—ultimately, against No. 1 Wake Forest itself.

The atmosphere in the Assembly Hall for that matchup with Wake Forest was like no night before. Call it magical. Amid that ocean of orange, there soon were no doubters. Then came the trip to the top of the polls, the long unbeaten streak, a Big Ten championship and the conference tournament title. Finally, the unnamed, orange-clad Illini were the No. 1 seed among No. 1 seeds, and the faithful filled the seats as Weber and Co. marched through Indy and back to Chicago.

There, with 4:04 remaining and a worthy Arizona opponent in control, the curtain started down. Then something happened. And then something else. Afterward, even the coaches and players were at a loss to describe it. Magic makes as much sense as anything.

Study every movement, every feint and flourish. You could still never quite describe it. But such was the season of 2004-05. At every practice and every performance, *News-Gazette* writers and photographers captured it for readers who just couldn't get enough of a team that captured both titles and hearts. I'm far from objective, but I think *The News-Gazette* sports staff is nearly without parallel. This book represents a tiny fraction of its collective effort over the course of one magical season.

ABOVE: **The 2004-05 team poses with the trophy after winning the Big Ten Conference tournament.** *Robert K. O'Daniell/The News-Gazette*

It's hard right now to imagine a time when the Assembly Hall no longer rings with the cry of "Dee for Threeee!" and no longer thrills in the power and precision of Deron, James, Luther and "the Rev." Perhaps this volume will help you remember the magic as it unfolded—right before your very eyes.

John Foreman
Editor and Publisher
The News-Gazette

Beyond X's and O's

Illini Look to Rewrite History in Year 100

BY LOREN TATE, *News-Gazette Columnist*

October 16, 2004

Hope springs like a gusher as Illini basketball reaches the century mark. Regardless of how often the winter campaigns end in a March train wreck, it is the unique aspect of Illini fans that they keep surging back for more.

They believe. Orange sweaters are out of winter storage. Orange blouses are pressed and carefully hung. Illini Nation is primed for another run. There is never the underlying pessimism, never the talk of jinxes or hexes—billy goats or The Babe—that seem to grip Chicago and Boston, even when home runs are flying in record numbers off lethal Cubs and Red Sox bats. There is never the underlying skepticism that, perhaps justifiably, clouds the Illini football picture.

Somehow, UI basketball fans aren't of a mind to expect the worst. And they've never been more charged up about a season than No. 100. Look what the Illini did in No. 99. They captured their first undisputed Big Ten championship since 1952 (fourth title won recently by three coaches), won 12 straight down the stretch and produced road triumphs at Purdue, Indiana and Iowa for the first time in 67 years. The NCAA tournament defeat of Cincinnati was a masterpiece, even if the follow-up 72-62 loss to Duke was not.

Positive outlook

So, here stand the Illini, 63-3 in the last five years at home and looking back on championships in which Lon Kruger won with Lou Henson recruits, Bill Self won with Kruger's products and Bruce Weber won with athletes brought in by Self. For those who preach the importance of continuity, Illinois has broken the mold. No other school in the country has dealt so successfully with this sort of coaching turnover.

Weber has an extra $150,000 in his bank account as the result of last season's successes, and he has all the pertinent members of his team returning. He has, if healthy, the equal of any guard trio in the nation in Deron Williams (Big Ten preseason Player of the Year), Dee Brown and Luther Head. They produced 38 points a game and handed out 407 assists last winter. The frontline is packed with experience with James Augustine and Roger Powell installed once again as the starters. In a sometimes-overlooked statistic, Powell shows a three-year field goal percentage of 58.8 percent, fourth on the career chart behind Illini legends Ken Norman (60.9), Deon Thomas (60.1) and Kenny Battle (59.1).

Clearly, Weber has a squad of thoroughbreds. However, this being the 100-year anniversary, we should be a little more mindful of history. The past would remind us to be wary of a program that, just when it seemed to be peaking, just when a national championship seemed possible, has been sidetracked by a world war, ineligibilities, sanctions, injuries, heartbreaking setbacks and a too-frequent inclination to go cold at tournament time.

What's past is past

It all began with four great juniors—Whiz Kids Gene Vance, Andy Phillip, Ken Menke and Jack Smiley—primed to win the NCAA title in 1943, when they were sadly broken up by military obligations. They returned a few years later, but it never happened.

Coach Harry Combes followed with a string of high-scoring teams in the 1950s that twice lost by two points in semifinal games … two of nine NCAA setbacks over the years by three points or fewer.

Some setbacks were unusual, to say the least. Combes' 1966-67 powerhouse was shattered by the "slush fund" scandal. Henson's Big Ten co-champs in 1984 were obliged to face Kentucky's Wildcats on their home court and came away disputing a midcourt call at the end. A good 1987 club must live forever with a 68-67 loss to Austin Peay. And what could be more unusual than the Illini being called for 56 personal fouls in an 87-81 loss to Arizona in 2001?

RIGHT: Dee Brown encourages the crowd as he joins his teammates on court during the Illini Madness festivities at the Assembly Hall. *John Dixon/The News-Gazette*

Dee, Deron & Co. chased off a lot of those demons last season. They gave all 10 conference rivals a taste of their bitter medicine. Using a comeback 51-49 triumph at Indiana as a springboard, they ran off a still-live streak of 10 conference victories. Particularly impressive were home wins against chief rivals Michigan State (75-51) and Wisconsin (65-57).

The Illini clinched the Big Ten title in Columbus, Ohio, and returned there for the NCAA tournament, where they blitzed Murray State 72-53 and Cincinnati 92-68. No wonder the orange-clad fandom is in a frenzy. With Gonzaga and Wake Forest coming up early, the latter December 1 at home, the Illini could go steamrolling toward Christmas with a legitimate shot at the nation's No. 1 ranking, a position they haven't held since briefly in 1989.

Those are giant thoughts but exactly the thoughts that ever-optimistic Illini Nation is thinking.

GAME 4   NOVEMBER 27, 2004

Conseco Fieldhouse, Indianapolis, Indiana

ILLINI PASS FIRST TEST OF SEASON WITH A+

BY BRETT DAWSON, *News-Gazette Staff Writer*

Maybe it was when Illinois' Roger Powell Jr. stepped backward, glanced at the three-point line, then calmly buried his first triple of the season. Maybe it was when Gonzaga big man Ronny Turiaf, stifled all afternoon, began berating his teammates out of frustration. Or, maybe it was the way Luther Head sped downcourt for a layup to beat the halftime buzzer.

Whatever sign you choose, it became apparent early that Illinois' supposed first test of this basketball season was nothing more than a pop quiz, an 89-72 rout of Gonzaga at the Wooden Tradition in Conseco Fieldhouse that was over by the half. The Illini popped jumpers, popped the ball from Turiaf and popped the Bulldogs on the jaw in what ultimately proved to be nothing more than one last study session for Wednesday's exam against Wake Forest.

"I think we were ready," Deron Williams said in the semester's biggest understatement. "It was our first time to play a team in the Top 25, and I think we came out to make a statement that we're for real."

How real? Real enough to hang 58 first-half points on Gonzaga. Real enough to sink a school-record-tying 14 three-pointers. Real enough to hold Turiaf—averaging 31 points a game entering the day—to an uneventful dozen on 4-of-10 shooting.

"I don't think they have a weakness at all," Bulldogs coach Mark Few said.

If they do, Gonzaga couldn't seem to find it. The next team to take a crack is the top-ranked Demon Deacons, 5-0 and fresh off a Preseason NIT title.

"We're going to find out how good we are on Wednesday," Bruce Weber said. "We controlled Gonzaga, but now can we control a game where the other team has great guards? It's a great test for us."

He says it like he means it. Of course, Weber also predicted Saturday would be a stern chal-

RIGHT: Dee Brown and Deron Williams combined for 37 points, 11 assists, eight three-pointers and four steals in the Illini's win over Gonzaga. *Mark Cowan/Icon SMI*

Illinois 89 | Gonzaga 72

lenge for his fifth-ranked Illini (4-0). It turned into Gonzaga's most lopsided regular-season loss since 1996. By halftime, it was a laugher, Illinois having buried 10 three-pointers—and the Zags—en route to a 58-27 lead.

"I love being up 30 at half," Weber said. "It's much easier to coach and much easier on the blood pressure."

But Weber admits he wasn't just expecting a test from Gonzaga, he was hoping for one. Though the Zags closed the game on a 32-15 run to make what once was a 38-point margin reasonably respectable, Illinois never was threatened. With the win, the Illini's average margin of victory dropped only slightly, to 24.7 points a game.

By contrast, Wake Forest had to escape Arizona 63-60 on Friday to win the Preseason NIT title at Madison Square Garden in New York. George Washington gave the Demon Deacons a game for a half in their season opener, and Providence fought hard in a 79-67 NIT semifinal result.

"They've had some challenges," Weber said. "And they've got veteran guys. They've been to Duke. They've been to (North) Carolina. So they're accustomed to going on the road and playing in big games. Part of you wishes we'd had a tougher game under our belt."

Gonzaga was supposed to provide that game. But Turiaf, who scored 40 points in a game last week against Idaho, never was a factor, and the Illini guards put the clamps on the Zags' inexperienced backcourt. In a fast-breaking, three-point-swishing first half, the Illini had leads of 18-4, 38-18 and 45-20.

Weber couldn't have predicted the lopsided margin, but the Illinois coach had a feeling his team was ready. They were "cut in"—a favorite Weberism for focused—during Thursday's and Friday's practices, and after routs of Delaware State, Florida A&M and Oakland, they were itching to play against a name opponent.

Weber's guard trio looked much too mature for Gonzaga's fresh-faced backcourt, combining for 57 points (the highest combined point total of their careers), 20 assists and eight steals. When Gonzaga tried to play man-to-man, Few's inexperienced backcourt of sophomore

	1st	2nd	Total
Illinois (#4)	58	31	89
Gonzaga (#25)	27	45	72

Illinois

Player	FGM-A	3FGM-A	FTM-A	O-D REB	A	BLK	S	TP
Augustine	3-8	0-0	0-0	3-2	2	3	1	6
Head	7-12	4-8	2-2	0-1	9	1	4	20
Williams	7-13	5-9	1-2	2-1	3	0	2	20
Brown	6-10	3-5	2-2	1-2	8	0	2	17
Smith	1-5	0-0	2-2	2-3	0	0	1	4
McBride	1-5	1-4	0-0	1-0	2	0	0	3
Ingram	1-3	0-0	0-0	0-4	0	2	1	2
Carter	2-8	0-1	0-0	3-1	0	0	0	4
Pruitt	1-2	0-0	0-0	0-0	0	0	1	2
Nkemdi	0-0	0-0	0-0	0-0	0	0	0	0
Totals	34-71 (47.9%)	14-28 (50.0%)	7-8 (87.5%)	14-15	24	6	13	89

Gonzaga

Player	FGM-A	3FGM-A	FTM-A	O-D REB	A	BLK	S	TP
Morrison	11-21	2-3	2-4	4-7	0	0	0	26
Mallon	2-9	0-1	3-6	3-4	1	1	1	7
Turiaf	4-10	0-1	4-4	3-6	4	4	0	12
Raivio	3-4	3-4	2-2	0-1	3	0	2	11
Doudney	1-2	1-2	0-0	1-2	0	1	1	3
Batista	4-10	0-1	2-2	3-1	1	0	0	10
Altidor-Cespedes	0-1	0-0	0-0	1-2	3	0	0	0
Pendergraft	0-0	0-0	3-4	1-0	0	0	0	3
Totals	25-57 (43.9%)	6-12 (50.0%)	16-22 (72.7%)	19-24	12	6	4	72

Derek Ravio and Texas Tech transfer Nathan Doudney couldn't keep up with Illinois' fleet-footed guards. When Few went to a zone, Illinois got in one from three-point range.

"We knew they could shoot the ball from three," Few said. "But they're so good at moving in their man-to-man that you're chasing them around and chasing them around. So you either get beat by the twos or you get beat by the threes."

RIGHT: Nick Smith shoots over defender Ronny Turiaf. Smith scored four points and grabbed five rebounds off the bench for the Illini. *Mark Cowan/Icon SMI*

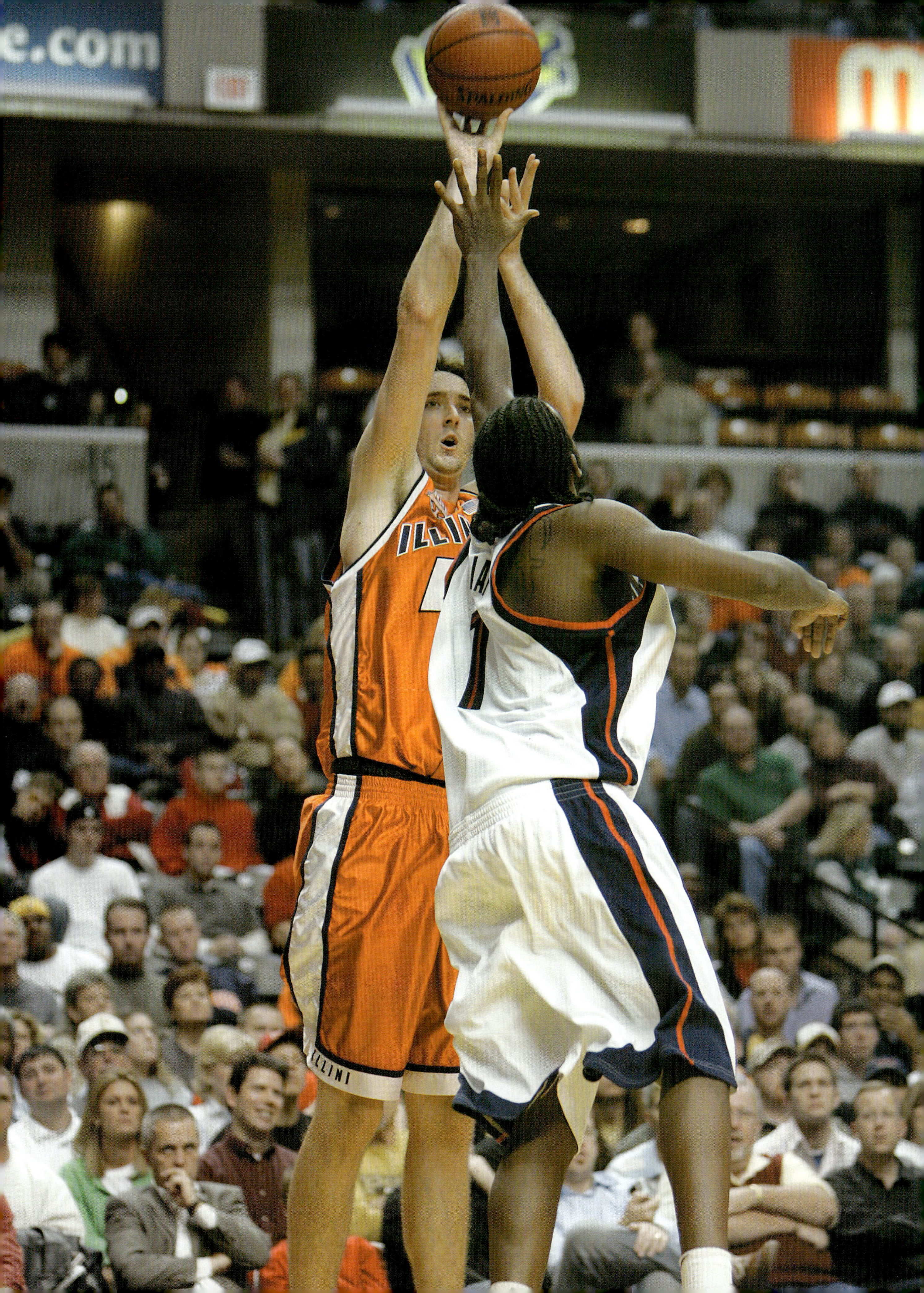
e.com
SPALDING
ILLINI
ILLINI

GAME 5   DECEMBER 1, 2004

Assembly Hall, Champaign, Illinois

ILLINI LEAVE NO. 1 DEACONS IN THEIR WAKE

BY BRETT DAWSON, *News-Gazette Staff Writer*

For one night, Champaign was the center of the basketball universe. And Illinois' 91-73 rout of Wake Forest on Wednesday provided one heck of a college hoops big bang.

The fans cheered—and "booed" and "Luuuued" and "Bruuuuced"—the band blared, and when the orange dust settled, Illinois had utterly dominated the nation's top-ranked team. The obvious question in the Wake (er, wake) of Illinois' destruction of the Demon Deacons: Is anybody better than the Illini?

"I don't know what to say," Illinois guard Dee Brown said. "After that performance, you tell me."

Ask the 16,618 hoarse fans who packed the Assembly Hall and chanted "We're No. 1" as the final seconds ticked. Ask the national audience that watched on ESPN. Or ask the Demon Deacons, who came in keepers of their first-ever No. 1 national ranking and left to echoes of "overrated!"

"If I had a vote?" Wake center Eric Williams said. "I'd put them No. 1 for sure."

Whether the Illini were good enough Wednesday night to catapult to that spot is up to coaches and writers who vote in the national polls. And it's up to the Arkansas Razorbacks, who get the opportunity to rain on this parade Saturday. But for one chilly December night, Illinois was the hottest team anywhere.

"It's not the end of the season," Illinois coach Bruce Weber said. "I hope we've got 30-something more games. It was a great test to see where we are. We performed well. But now there's a lot more tests to come."

The thing is, Illinois can't seem to get tested. Wake Forest came to town as part of the ACC/Big Ten Challenge. "Challenge" is right there in the name. But the game was a laugher before halftime. Even with Luther Head's 80-foot heave (barely) missing at the first-half

---

RIGHT: Dee Brown reacts to the crowd during Illinois' stunning victory over Wake Forest. *John Dixon/The News-Gazette*

Illinois 91 | Wake Forest 73

buzzer, Illinois led 54-33 and never was threatened.

The Illini are winning their games by an average of 23.4 points. Their last two opponents—both ranked when the games tipped off—have lost by a combined 35 points.

"They haven't had any game pressure all year," Wake Forest coach Skip Prosser said. "We had it to 17 with a wide-open three, and maybe (if) we make that it puts a little game pressure on them. We didn't, then they make a three and it was all damage control after that."

Illinois did plenty of damage, hitting 11 three-pointers, dishing out 27 assists and leading by as many as 32 points. The Illini did plenty of controlling, too, holding Wake's heralded backcourt duo of Chris Paul and Justin Gray to 21 points—almost 10 below their combined average—on 7-for-27 shooting.

They got balance (19 points from Roger Powell Jr., 16 each from Brown and Head) and gave their coach little room for complaint.

"The first half, when it was key, we had the edge on the rebounds," Weber said. "We were good in the offense, we were good on the Matto (hustle) chart. We were pretty good tonight."

Maybe as good as anybody has been this season. Prosser passed on the chance to anoint Illinois the nation's new No. 1 team, saying he hasn't seen enough of the competition to hold a coronation. And the Illini mostly dodged the question of whether they're the nation's best team.

"I'm gonna leave that up to you (media) guys," Head said. "Y'all are going to do your job, I hope. We're just going to keep playing hard."

They're also playing hard to catch. Illinois has played 200 minutes this season. It's trailed for seven minutes and 51 seconds. The Illini never gave up the lead against Wake Forest.

"We made a statement that we are pretty good," Brown said. "We're one of the best teams, if not the best, in the Big Ten. Hopefully we're one of those teams that are going to make some noise come March."

	1st	2nd	Total
Wake Forest (#1)	33	40	73
Illinois (#3)	54	37	91

Wake Forest

Player	FGM-A	3FGM-A	FTM-A	O-D REB	A	BLK	S	TP
Levy	3-8	0-2	0-0	5-2	4	0	1	6
Danelius	2-5	1-3	0-1	1-3	1	0	0	5
Williams	7-13	0-0	4-6	1-5	1	0	0	18
Gray	3-16	3-8	2-2	2-1	2	0	0	11
Paul	4-11	1-3	1-1	1-4	6	0	2	10
Ellis	0-0	0-0	0-0	0-0	0	0	0	0
Downey	4-8	4-7	0-0	0-4	4	0	0	12
Joyce	2-2	1-1	2-2	1-0	0	0	0	7
Feather	0-0	0-0	0-0	0-0	0	0	0	0
Strickland	0-0	0-0	0-0	0-0	0	0	0	0
Buck	0-0	0-0	0-0	0-0	0	0	0	0
Visser	2-5	0-0	0-0	1-3	0	0	0	4
Totals	27-68	10-24	9-12	13-24	18	0	3	73
	(39.7%)	(41.7%)	(75.0%)					

Illinois

Player	FGM-A	3FGM-A	FTM-A	O-D REB	A	BLK	S	TP
Head	6-14	4-6	0-0	0-5	5	0	1	16
Powell Jr.	8-10	2-2	1-1	3-4	0	0	0	19
Augustine	4-4	0-0	2-2	2-5	0	3	1	10
Williams	4-10	0-4	0-0	0-5	11	0	1	8
Brown	7-12	2-6	0-0	1-5	7	0	0	16
McBride	3-6	3-6	0-0	0-1	2	0	0	9
Carter	2-3	0-1	0-1	0-0	0	0	1	4
Smith	2-5	0-1	1-2	0-3	2	0	0	5
Ingram	1-2	0-0	0-0	1-0	0	0	0	2
Pruitt	1-1	0-0	0-0	0-0	0	0	0	2
Nkemdi	0-1	0-0	0-0	0-0	0	0	0	0
Totals	38-68	11-26	4-6	7-30	27	3	4	91
	(55.9%)	(42.3%)	(66.7%)					

And March is where the Illini are keeping one eye. Weber reiterated in his postgame news conference that his goal is to have a No. 1 or No. 2 seed for the NCAA tournament, and he called Wednesday's win "a big step" toward achieving that goal.

But it was more than that, he admitted. It was a showcase for his program, a game that had been hyped since the start of the season and a matchup widely regarded as the best the ACC/Big Ten Challenge had to offer. In short, it was a commercial for the Illini. And Weber rolled out a winning product.

"…We did well," Weber said, "but that doesn't mean we're a finished product. At least I hope not."

RIGHT: **Coach Bruce Weber, sporting an orange blazer, had his team ready for Wake Forest on "Paint the Hall Orange" night.** *John Dixon/The News-Gazette*

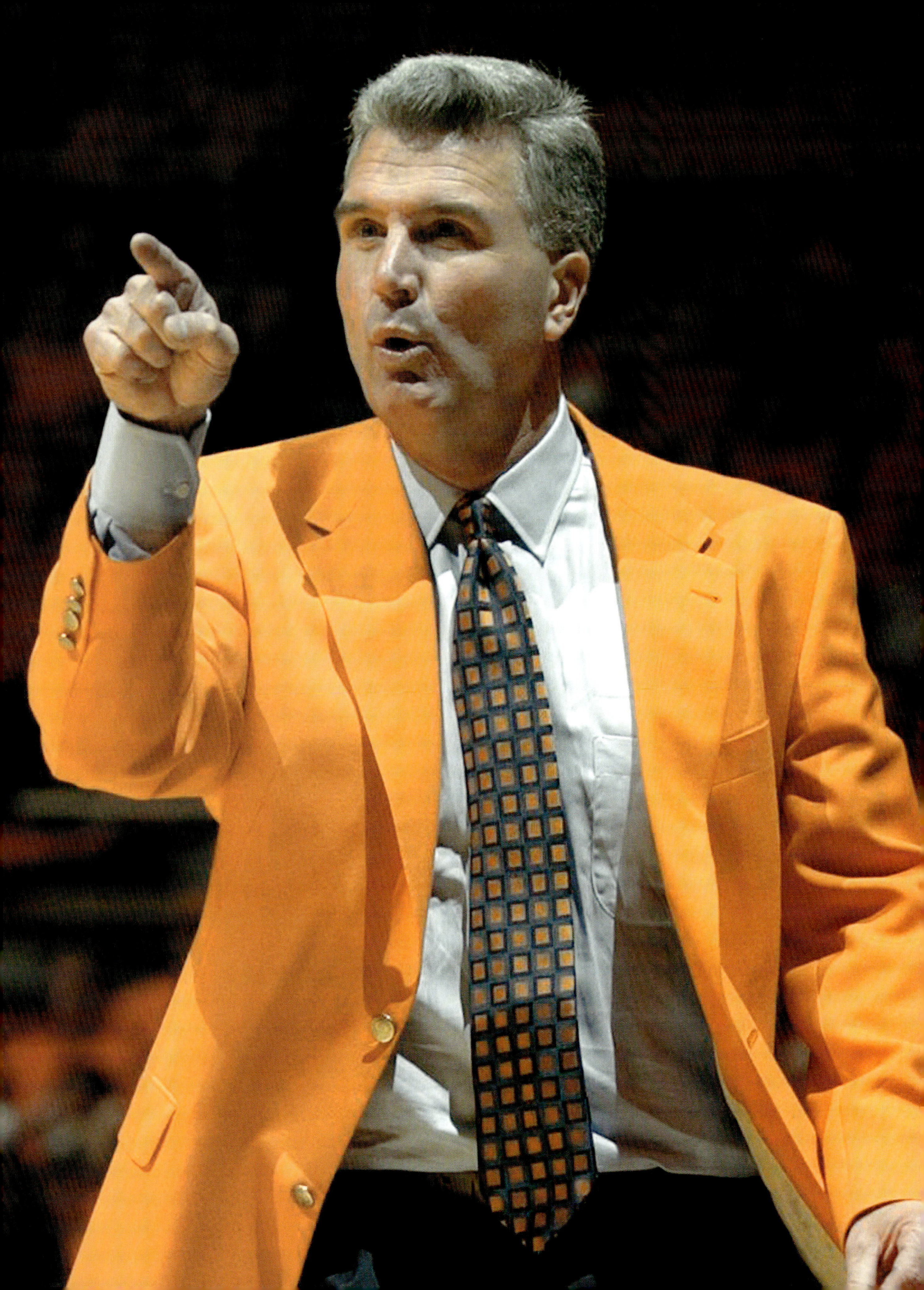

BIG WIN, BUT NOT THAT BIG

BY LOREN TATE, *News-Gazette Columnist*

December 1, 2004

It's not a fluke if you keep repeating it.

Fresh from another offensive explosion Bruce Weber's whirlwind Illini compiled another set of incredible numbers.

An Illini club that built a 38-point lead on Gonzaga returned home to put the Wake Forest Demon Deacons on the ropes by 32 in a 91-73 result.

In 100 years of UI basketball, no team ever has put forth such remarkable first-half numbers through the first five games. Illinois is averaging more than 53 points in five opening halves while shooting 59 percent from the field and draining 41 of 79 three-pointers.

The most difficult aspect of Weber's job is getting his starters ready for the second half. These games are already over by then. This was less of a concern Wednesday because fouls limited Deron Williams to eight minutes in a scoreless half, so he returned with a fever.

Yep, that's right. Illinois scored 54 first-half points with none from the Big Ten's preseason MVP. He came on strong, handing out 11 assists as he, Luther Head and Dee Brown combined for 23 assists, 16 rebounds and 40 points (note the order; assists come first with these guys).

The hottest new argument, particularly from the metropolitan and national visitors who clogged the media spots, is which of the UI's three guards is the best. It was Dee on Wednesday. Or was it Luther?

Nice Night

Where does Wednesday's game fit among the Assembly Hall's featured contests? It's big because fans perceived it that way. From the standpoint of hype, it's off the charts.

But let's be a killjoy for a moment. For starters, Coach Skip Prosser repeatedly pointed out that Wake Forest hadn't played enough games to deserve the No. 1 ranking, and he was correct. Secondly, the fact that the game was over at halftime detracts from it as a historical icon. The orange-clad caldron, as Prosser called it, kept cheering out of habit, not excitement.

Finally, these home blowouts against quality foes are becoming routine in the Illini's 67-for-70 run at the Assembly Hall. Michigan State's last two trips here resulted in 75-51 and 70-40 UI romps. Two years ago on December 3, North Carolina was obliterated, 92-65, and Indiana's Hoosiers, one year removed from an NCAA runner-up finish, bowed here 80-54. Wisconsin's Big Ten co-champs in 2002 were stunned 80-48.

This was excitement for a day, but the ease of the triumph ultimately will detract from it. The touted guard showdown was no contest.

RIGHT: Deron Williams dribbles past defender Chris Paul. The heavily touted guard matchup between Illinois and Wake Forest was easily won by the Illini.
John Dixon/The News-Gazette

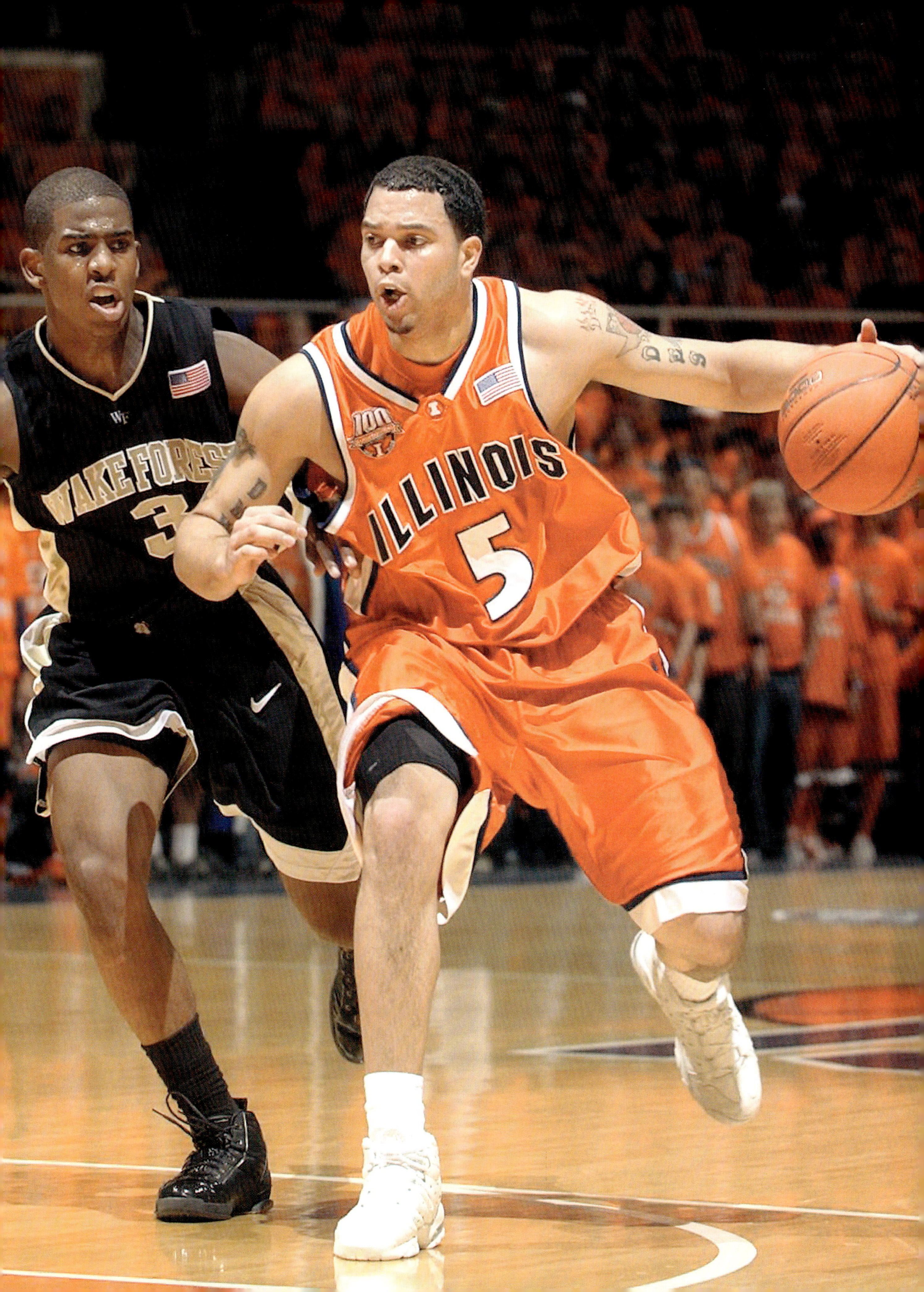
ILLINOIS
5
WAKE FOREST
3

Beyond X's and O's

"The Rev"

BY BRETT DAWSON, *News-Gazette Staff Writer*

October 10, 2004

Roger Powell Jr. unlocks the door and asks, before you can slide into the passenger seat of his charcoal-gray Chrysler, "You like gospel music?" You had better be able to tolerate the non-secular stuff these days if you intend to ride shotgun with Illinois' senior forward. There aren't a lot of other options. Not since last spring.

"It's Israel and New Breed," Powell says of the soulful sounds that spill out of his considerable system. "Ever heard of them?"

As Powell wheels his sleek LHS—license plate: "AIR ROG 2"—onto Kirby Avenue, he reaches into his wallet and produces a laminated card. At the top, printed in detailed caligraphy, is the name of his church back home in Joliet—Mt. Zion Full Gospel Tabernacle. Looks like a business card. In a way, it is.

"I just got it yesterday," a proud Powell says, turning down the volume on the stereo with the touch of a slender remote control. "I'm not ordained yet, but I will be."

The card is Powell's minister's license. This ride has taken an unexpected turn. It's a little like Roger Powell's life in that way.

Turn for the Better

The story you are supposed to be reading is about how Powell made an ill-advised—and much-criticized—decision last spring to enter the NBA draft and didn't tell his coach, Bruce Weber. Instead, this is the story of a 21-year-old who six months ago reached a crossroads.

And Powell? He took the road less traveled. Those gospel CDs in the car are the only ones left after a hip-hop purge last spring.

"I threw out a ton of CDs," Powell says. "The day after I saw *The Passion of the Christ*, matter of fact. I was just like, 'Jesus did all this for me, and I'm listening to this stuff?' It really affected me."

Drinking? He'll have water, thanks, with lemon and lime. Cursing? Gosh, no. This is the brand-new Roger Powell Jr., and the path here has been long and winding.

"It's weird, man," Powell says as he pilots his ride down a short stretch of Neil Street. "But it's awesome, too. Everything has changed."

It changed last spring, though Powell is reluctant to say why. He was going through "some things," he says, and does not elaborate. That's when the signs started. They came around the time Illinois was playing in the 2004 NCAA tournament, and today, though Powell is happy to discuss his faith as he settles into a booth at the back of TGI Friday's, he's reluctant to talk about the signs.

"I'm not sure people will understand," he says.

Why would they? Powell himself didn't, at first. He couldn't comprehend why, when a question would come into his mind at church, the answer would come immediately in a pastor's sermon. Or why, when he was watching the Trinity Broadcast Network, the day's topic would fall so closely in line with what was going on in his own life. And that was only the beginning.

ABOVE: Roger Powell Jr. poses at his local church of worship, Church of the Living God. *Robert K. O'Daniell/The News-Gazette*

"It's hard to explain, but people would come up to me—people I didn't know—and they would say, 'God has something for you,'" Powell says. "I started to understand that it was my calling."

He had ignored it long enough.

Typical Teenager

Cherry Powell didn't raise a bad seed. The wife of Roger Sr. and mother of Roger Jr. took her son to church every Sunday, and though she and her husband didn't force religion on their son, she knew him to be a spiritual child from an early age. But the teenage years have a way of testing a mother's faith.

"He was never a bad kid, but he did the things teenagers do," Cherry Powell says. "Drinking and things. He was like anybody else, sneaking out trying to do those things—and getting in trouble with me."

Still, Powell attended Sunday service. Every week. In high school, he was a good student as well as a basketball star at Joliet. And even as he acted out the way teenagers do, he left hints that he someday might heed a higher calling.

"He always had the people of God in his heart," says Craig Purchase, Powell's longtime pastor at Mt. Zion Full Tabernacle. "When they asked him his goals in life, he would say he wanted to build a church for the people of God."

He also wanted to be a basketball star. And, Cherry says, he wanted the trappings that came with it.

"The girls," she says. "That was always the thing for him. … That's why he ran from the ministry.

"It was always calling him. He just didn't always listen."

A Faith-Filled Journey

But Powell never fully tuned out the message. Shortly after he settled in Champaign, he set out to "find a spiritual home," and as an

Illinois freshman, he found it at the Church of the Living God, a lively little spot on Fourth Street with bright red pews and the words "Praise the Lord!" hung on a wall below the cross. He got to know Bishop Lloyd Gwin. He became a regular on Sundays. Okay, a semi-regular.

"I'm not going to lie—when I first came here, I missed a few Sundays," Powell says, fidgeting with a lime wedge. "I was at college. I had never been away from home in my life. I wanted to go out a little bit on the weekends, have some fun."

But the deeper he went into his college career, the more deeply Powell was drawn into his faith. His sophomore year, teammate Brian Cook introduced him to the Fellowship of Christian Athletes and Kent Hollis, that organization's local representative.

"He was obviously a Christian young man," Hollis says. "But I didn't know how sincere he was about his faith."

Hollis soon found out. Not long after Powell first joined his teammates in Bible discussions with Hollis, he began speaking to kids at FCA-sponsored events. He talked about building a relationship with God, and he was surprised at how easily the words came to him. But while Powell believed in the message he was delivering, and while he had become a mainstay at Sunday services in Champaign, outside of church, he was just a typical college kid with a basketball scholarship.

"I went out," Powell said. "I drank. I wasn't a bad guy or anything. It's just that, in retrospect to where I am now, I wasn't living a holy life."

"The Rev"

Now, Powell is living what he considers a holy life. What he's trying to avoid is living a holier-than-thou life. Those close to Powell are aware that some will question his decision. But ask the man himself if he's prepared for negative feedback, and he glances at you as if he's misunderstood the question.

"How could anyone see this as a bad thing?" he asks.

His teammates agree.

"We call him 'The Rev' now," says Dee Brown, never one to back down about speaking his mind. "He's giving himself over to God. That's a positive thing. It's not easy. I wish I could do it."

Weber has noticed a change in Powell since his decision to enter the ministry. But he's also noticed that Powell "hasn't gone overboard," with regard to preaching his own lifestyle, an important distinction in maintaining team harmony.

As for basketball? Weber isn't worried about Powell's priorities.

"I think he's always had a strong faith, and now it's just that he's going to make that his future," Weber says. "If anything, I think he's been more focused toward the season and on getting better."

Improving on the Court, too

For all his considerable talent on a basketball court, Powell is, as of today, considered a marginal NBA prospect. Chris Monter, who publishes the *Monter Draft News*, says he likely wouldn't have been selected in either the first or second round of last spring's draft, and that NBA scouts will need to see some perimeter skills out of Powell before they'd consider spending a 2005 selection on him.

"We talk all the time about how the NBA isn't a club they just invite you to," Weber says. "We tell him, 'If you want to make it, then go work on your ball handling, your shooting, your defense. If you want it, go work at it.'"

So Powell has worked. For hours on end. Shooting free throws. Putting up jump shots. Dribbling with both hands. Until a minor hamstring injury slowed him last week, he was perhaps Illinois' most diligent offseason worker.

That's always been his way. It hasn't changed since he heard his calling.

"He still has aspirations of the NBA, and we still encourage that," Cherry Powell says. "And I think this will open up that path. I always tell him, 'If you're not true to everything in your life, don't expect other things to be true to you.'

ABOVE: Roger Powell Jr. decorates his game-day shoes with reminders of his faith.
Robin Scholz/The News-Gazette

By accepting the ministry, I think his NBA aspirations now are even more possible."

Staying the Course

Beyond the studying and the preaching, though, Powell also will need to stay on what Weber calls a "pretty straight and narrow path." Those close to Powell say he's up to that task.

Last spring, when he threw out those CDs, his mother asked, "Why don't you give them to some friends of yours who still listen to that stuff, as gifts?"

"He looked at me and said, 'Why would I want to say, 'I'm not going to listen to this anymore, but then give it to them to listen to?'" Cherry Powell says. "And you know what? He was right. It would be like giving you a bottle of wine and saying, 'But my body is clean.'"

Powell's body is clean. His mind, too. And he has no intention of changing that any time soon.

"On my own, this would be hard," Powell says. "But when God came into it? It all got so easy. It wasn't hard to give up those things I used to do because God was there to help me."

A few days after that ride to TGI Friday's, Powell is dressed for a photo shoot. He smiles for the camera, and, surprised to have wrapped up so quickly he asks, "You want to go get lunch again?"

I wish that I could but tell him, regretfully, that I can't. I have a deadline, and I'm expecting phone calls.

"No, that's cool," Powell says. "I can go eat by myself."

With that, and a friendly handshake, he slips into that Chrysler of his and drives off, a man clearly comfortable with going his own way.

We thank the Fighting Illini for this season's heart pounding excitement.

The entire staff from the Provena Central Illinois Region congratulates the University of Illinois Basketball Team and Coaches for their great year on the court. We salute the dedication and the sheer talent that helped create such an enjoyable, successful basketball season.

PROVENA
Covenant
Medical Center
www.provenacovenant.org

PROVENA
United Samaritans
Medical Center
www.provenausmc.com

More Pay for your Play

Now offering even *more* benefits & rewards in **2005**!

Prime Rewards.
FREE to join, FREE to use!

Subject to modification or cancellation without notice. See Par-A-Dice for complete details.

If you or someone you know has a gambling problem, crisis counseling and referral services can be accessed by calling 1-800-GAMBLER (1-800-426-2537).

FREE Admission!

PAR·A·DICE HOTEL·CASINO

E. Peoria, IL • 1-800-Par-A-Dice • www.par-a-dice.com   BOYD GAMING

GAME 11   DECEMBER 22, 2004

Savvis Center, St. Louis, Missouri

WINNING THE BORDER WAR PROVES TOUGH

BY BRETT DAWSON, *News-Gazette Staff Writer*

It's supposed to be the other reason to celebrate this week, cause to parade around the court, maybe to pop a cork or two. A reason to party. But Illinois' post-Braggin' Rights celebration here Wednesday, after a 70-64 win against Missouri, was relatively tame.

"We're happy to win," Illini guard Deron Williams said after his team continued its stranglehold on the series, winning a fifth straight against the Tigers. "Mostly, we're tired."

The Illini will celebrate this week with their families, unwrapping presents and feasting on home-cooked food. On Wednesday, though, they left the merriment to the orange-clad among the 22,153 fans in the Savvis Center.

Fact is, the top-ranked Illini (11-0) didn't feel much like celebrating. Not after their hardest-fought, most physical victory of the season. It was uglier than the Illini hoped. It was closer than anyone expected.

And it was tiring.

"I think they enjoyed getting the trophy, they enjoyed the atmosphere," Illinois coach Bruce Weber said. "But we got in the locker room and it was more like a relief."

Small wonder. Illinois, a model of offensive efficiency all season, shot like someone spiked the nog, tying a season low by shooting 42.3 percent from the floor and firing mostly blanks (5 of 20) from three-point range. And though Illinois' defense was mostly steady, limiting Mizzou to 37.7 percent shooting, it was wobbly enough to allow Tigers sophomore Linas Kleiza a 25-point night. So, hold off on the fireworks.

The Illini were smiling when the buzzer sounded, but the ear-to-ear grins you've come to associate with a Braggin' Rights win were hard to find in the postgame.

"We're happy to get a win, yeah, but we didn't play our best basketball," said forward Roger Powell Jr., who battled Kleiza and foul trouble and finished with 14 points. "Any time

---

RIGHT: James Augustine battles for a rebound against Missouri. *Darrell Hoemann/The News-Gazette*

Illinois 70 | Missouri 64

one guy scores 25 on you, you can't be happy about that. We have some things to work on."

But not today. For a few days, at least, Weber and his players will focus their attentions elsewhere. They'll scatter for the holiday, some heading to Champaign, others to their families' homes. But they'll come back to practice Sunday with work to do.

"If we had lost, it would have been hard to enjoy Christmas, but you still have to value the time you have with your family," said Williams, who sat out last season's Braggin' Rights game with a broken jaw but on Wednesday had 19 points and five assists.

Weber will focus on fine-tuning his team's motion offense. And he'll show his players the film of Wednesday's game, of how for the first time this season they didn't make the extra pass, didn't stay in constant movement at the offensive end.

"I thought defensively we were pretty good," Weber said. "We just have some things we can tighten up offensively."

Weber wasn't ready to push the panic button, not after a win against his biggest nonconference rival. Still, the Illini weren't perfect. After building a 15-point halftime lead, they allowed a 6-5 team that's struggled offensively all season to creep back into a game.

Hardly reason enough, Weber said, for a blue Christmas. Not on a night when Luther Head scored 20 points, Illinois stared down foul trouble and survived and the Illini won for the 25th time in 27 games.

"We still won," Weber said. "We made free throws, we took care of the basketball and made enough plays down the stretch. I think everybody's a little disillusioned by all the other scores. But at the same time, did we play great basketball? No."

His players recognized that fact.

"I think we have a higher standard this year, so even though we're happy, we know we could've been better," Williams said. "But I think that's a good thing."

So does Weber, who was happy not only to have a game film with which to instruct his players on what they're doing wrong, but was also pleased that his players' postgame celebration was tempered with a dose of disappointment.

"If they're satisfied with this tonight, somebody's going to catch up to us," Weber said. "I think it's good to hit some rough bumps in the way."

It's even better, the Illini said, to do it with a win.

	1st	2nd	Total
Illinois (#1)	38	32	70
Missouri	23	41	64

Illinois

Player	FGM-A	3FGM-A	FTM-A	O-D REB	A	BLK	S	TP
Augustine	1-3	0-0	0-1	2-2	1	1	0	2
Powell Jr.	4-5	1-2	5-8	2-4	0	2	0	14
Head	6-14	2-7	6-6	2-5	2	0	4	20
Williams	5-13	1-3	8-10	0-3	5	1	1	19
Brown	4-11	1-5	2-2	0-4	5	0	3	11
McBride	0-1	0-1	0-0	0-1	0	0	0	0
Smith	1-2	0-0	0-0	2-2	0	0	0	2
Ingram	1-3	0-1	0-0	1-1	0	0	0	2
Totals	22-52	5-19	21-27	13-22	13	4	8	70
	(42.3%)	(26.3%)	(77.8%)					

Missouri

Player	FGM-A	3FGM-A	FTM-A	O-D REB	A	BLK	S	TP
Young	2-7	0-0	1-5	7-1	0	0	0	5
Kleiza	6-11	2-4	11-13	3-4	3	1	1	25
McKinney	3-6	0-1	2-3	0-5	2	0	1	8
Conley	0-3	0-1	2-2	2-3	0	0	1	2
Horton	3-7	2-4	0-1	0-2	4	0	2	8
Gardner	3-11	2-6	0-0	2-1	0	0	0	8
Laurie	0-1	0-1	0-0	0-0	0	0	0	0
Brown	3-6	1-1	1-1	0-1	0	0	0	8
Dandridge	0-0	0-0	0-0	0-0	0	0	0	0
Grimes	0-1	0-0	0-0	0-1	0	0	0	0
Totals	20-53	7-18	17-25	17-21	9	1	5	64
	(37.7%)	(38.9%)	(68.0%)					

RIGHT: Luther Head came up huge for the Illini in their win over Missouri with 20 points, seven rebounds and four steals. *Darrell Hoemann/The News-Gazette*

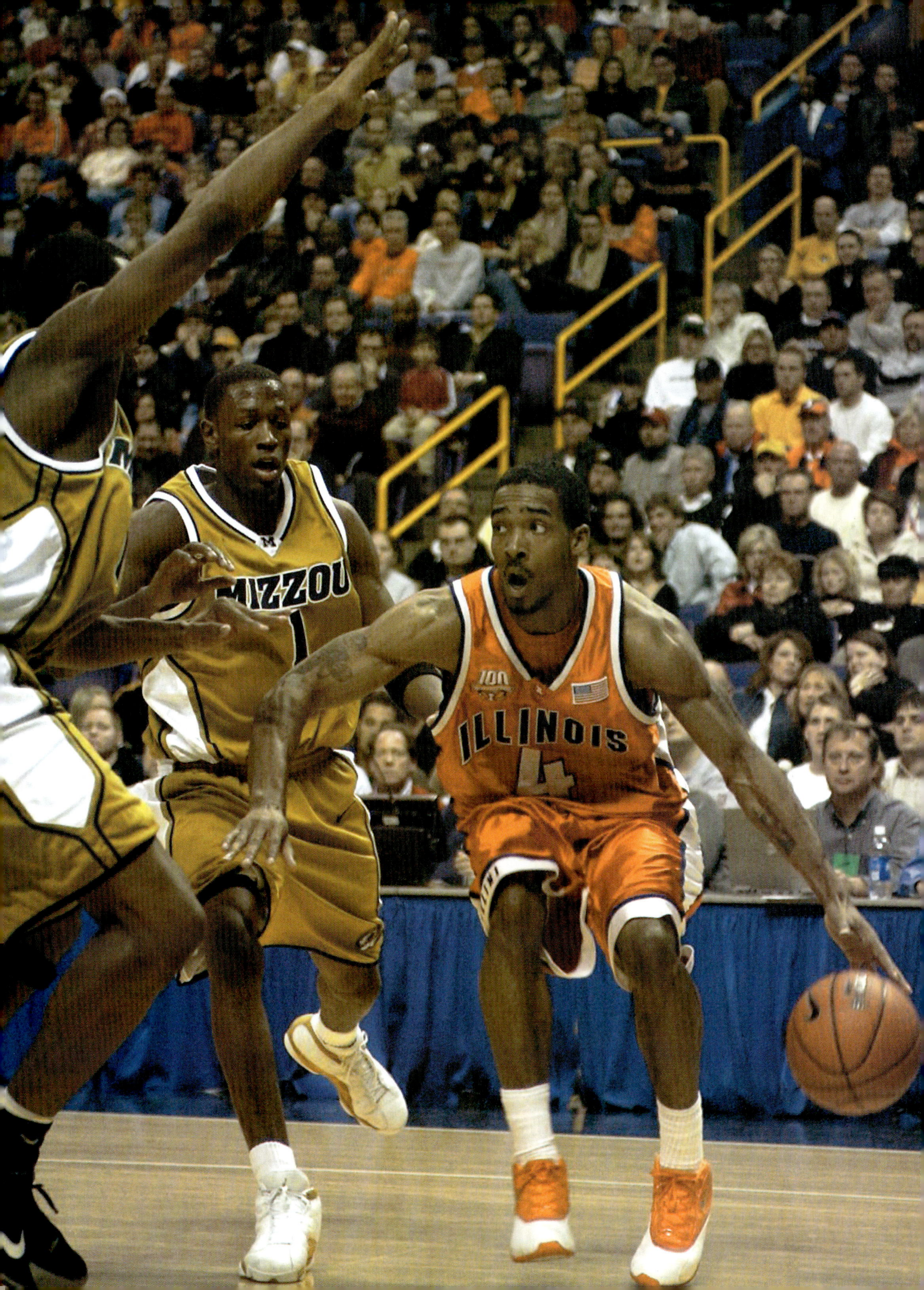
MIZZOU
1
ILLINOIS
4

GAME 14 DECEMBER 31, 2004
Valley High School, Las Vegas, Nevada

ILLINI WIN WITH HUSTLE— AND MUSCLE

BY BRETT DAWSON, *News-Gazette Staff Writer*

It would be a great story. Bruce Weber scrawls "14-0" on a dry erase board before Illinois' first basketball game of the season. He tells his players the odds are long, the competition tough, but he wants to go undefeated in the non-conference schedule.

It would be a great story. But it's not entirely true.

"Actually, he wrote 13-0," Illinois guard Deron Williams said Friday night, after Illinois rang out the old year with a 67-45 thumping of Cincinnati in the title game of the Las Vegas Holiday Classic. "A couple of days ago, he figured out that it was 14 and he started talking about that."

That's about the only thing Weber's done wrong this season. Make it 14-0 for the Illini, their first perfect pre-conference run since 1989-90. With that out of the way, the New Year's resolution is simple: Win the Big Ten.

Illinois certainly is prepared for it. Cincinnati saw to that, trying to override the Illini's hustle with its muscle. But the previously unbeaten Bearcats (11-1) found an Illinois team unwilling to back down from a bump. And, in a case of turnabout being foul play, the Illini gave as good as they got.

"They were crying to the refs for fouls," said Illinois guard Dee Brown, whose 13 points pushed him to 1,010 for his career. "They said we were too physical."

Regardless of who was the more physical team, there was little doubt when the buzzer sounded as far as which one was the best. Illinois, which had humbled Cincinnati 92-68 last season in a run-and-fun NCAA tournament tilt, proved it had the mettle to match its pedal-to-the-metal pace. When it was over, the Illini felt they'd gotten over one more hurdle in the search for the national championship.

"It shows you we can play different styles," said Luther Head, the tournament MVP after an

---

RIGHT: The tiny gym at Valley High School in Las Vegas could barely contain the energy of Illinois' "one-man fast break," Dee Brown. *AP/WWP*

Illinois 67 | Cincinnati 45

11-point performance on Friday. "We didn't make shots like we did last year (against Cincinnati), but we still came out and played aggressive and did what we had to do to win."

Call it ugly if you will. The Illini call it justification of a rep long forgotten. There was a time when Illinois was known for physical, grind-it-out basketball. Most of these players were recruited to a style that's up-tempo by Big Ten standards, but hardly pure finesse.

"If people have forgotten that we're a physical team, I hope they keep forgetting," Brown said. "We'll hit them with some muscle and they won't be ready for it."

Even Weber couldn't have imagined how thoroughly his team would dominate its competition, winning 13 of its 14 non-conference games by double digits and outscoring opponents by an average of 20.6 points per game. They've done it with blistering offensive runs, unselfish passing (a whopping 20.6 assists per game) and a defense that here in Vegas got back to its grimy roots, holding Cincinnati to 28 percent shooting. And they've done it against a schedule that, while hardly murderous, is no pushover, either. Four of Illinois' 14 victims—Wake Forest, Arkansas, Oregon and now Cincinnati—haven't lost to anyone else. Another, Gonzaga, has only one other loss.

The Bearcats, still steamed after what they called an embarrassing NCAA tournament loss, were supposed to be the team with the muscle and the motivation to end Illinois' streak. But even from the opening minutes, when Brown swiped an inbound pass for a layup-and-foul that resulted in a three-point play and a 7-2 lead, Cincinnati hardly seemed like a threat.

The game was Illinois' third this season against a ranked opponent. The outcome of those three games never was in doubt in the second half.

"We've played different styles, different kinds of teams, but really the defense has led the way," Weber said. "Against Wake Forest and Gonzaga, it led to easy buckets. Tonight, we defended so well, and we rebounded with them, which is key. That's their forte."

	1st	2nd	Total
Cincinnati (#17)	24	21	45
Illinois (#1)	35	32	67

Cincinnati

Player	FGM-A	3FGM-A	FTM-A	O-D REB	A	BLK	S	TP
Hicks	3-8	0-1	2-8	3-5	1	1	2	8
Kirkland	1-8	1-2	2-2	0-1	1	1	0	5
Maxiell	3-8	0-0	6-10	6-5	1	2	0	12
Moore	2-7	2-5	0-0	0-2	0	0	0	6
White	2-3	0-1	0-2	0-2	2	1	2	4
Muhammad	2-12	0-3	2-2	3-1	0	0	2	6
Williams	1-3	1-3	1-2	1-4	0	0	0	4
Lucas	0-0	0-0	0-0	0-0	1	0	0	0
Bright	0-1	0-0	0-1	0-0	0	0	0	0
Totals	14-50 (28.0%)	4-15 (26.7%)	13-26 (50.0%)	16-23	6	5	6	45

Illinois

Player	FGM-A	3FGM-A	FTM-A	O-D REB	A	BLK	S	TP
Augustine	1-3	0-0	1-2	2-3	1	0	0	3
Powell Jr.	5-10	0-0	3-4	4-0	2	0	2	13
Head	4-11	2-5	1-2	1-7	3	0	1	11
Williams	6-15	3-8	3-4	0-6	4	0	0	18
Brown	4-7	3-6	2-3	2-3	2	0	3	13
McBride	1-3	1-2	0-0	0-1	0	0	0	3
Smith	1-4	0-0	2-2	0-2	2	0	0	4
Ingram	0-1	0-1	2-2	2-1	0	1	0	2
Nkemdi	0-0	0-0	0-0	1-0	0	0	0	0
Carter	0-1	0-0	0-0	1-0	0	0	0	0
Pruitt	0-1	0-0	0-0	0-0	0	0	0	0
Totals	22-56 (39.3%)	9-22 (40.9%)	14-19 (73.7%)	13-26	14	1	6	67

Illinois' forte these days is winning. Just like Weber hoped. In the locker room after the game, Weber's players talked about the three seasons—pre-conference, Big Ten play and post-season—and how dominating the first is only phase one of a master plan. And that's the next motivational message the Illinois coach intends to send.

"We can't let this be the end," Weber said. "This has got to be a start."

RIGHT: Roger Powell Jr. slams home two of his 13 points against the Bearcats. *AP/WWP*

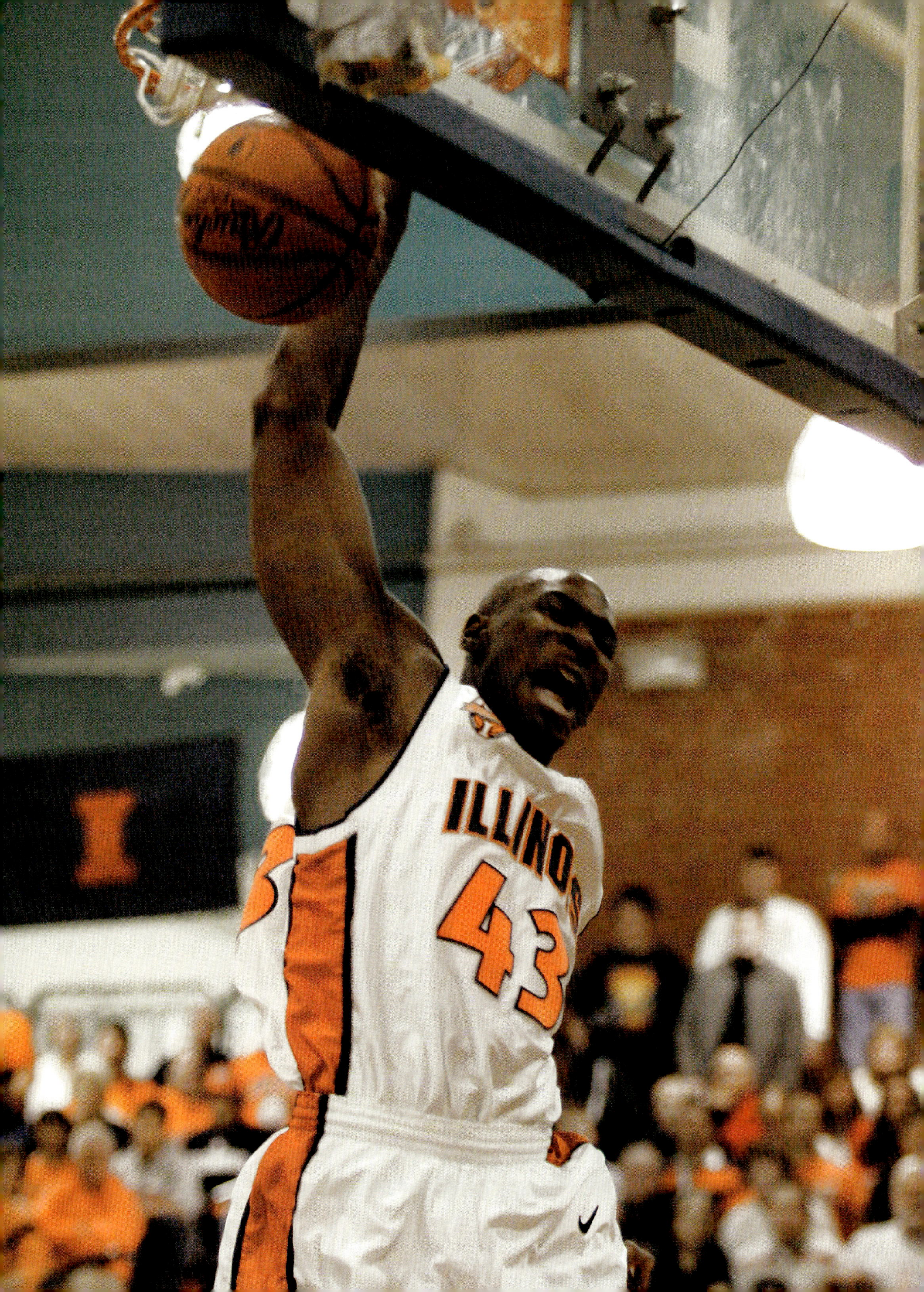
ILLINOIS
43

Beyond X's and O's

Three of a Kind

BY BRETT DAWSON, *News-Gazette Staff Writer*

January 23, 2005

Luther Head slumps down in his chair. Gets comfortable. He has a feeling he could be here for a while. The question has just been posed to Head, Dee Brown and Deron Williams: "When was the last time you guys got into an argument?" The answer, naturally, has led to an argument.

"We argue over everything," Williams says, pointing to Brown. "He still thinks (Allen) Iverson is the best player in the (NBA)."

Head rolls his eyes.

"Whenever a guy's 5-11 and he's got to be double-teamed, he's special," Brown says, his voice raising a decibel.

Head covers his face with his right hand.

"You wanted an argument, you got it," Head says. "They'll go on like this the whole time if you let 'em."

And sure enough, they do go on a good while, Williams listing a string of All-Stars he claims are better than Iverson: "Tim Duncan, Kevin Garnett, Tracy McGrady ..."

"You saw T-Mac live in person," Brown says. "He's 6-9. I'm talking about a dude 5-11 ..."

But Williams is undeterred: "Kevin Garnett, Kobe (Bryant), LeBron (James) ..."

"You would not take Kobe over Iverson," Brown says, disbelief apparent.

Head just laughs.

"They always do this," he says.

He should know. If Illinois' backcourt were the Beatles—and the on-court music Head, Brown and Williams have made this season lives up to the comparison—then Head is George. The quiet one.

Brown and Williams? They're John and Paul, pre-Yoko.

"It's always arguing and this and that, and then it's over," Head says. "I just sit back and watch."

Hearing this, Williams stops arguing with Brown.

"And that's another thing: Why does everybody think Luther is so quiet?" Williams says. "He has a quiet voice. He talks like a little girl. Other than that, there's nothing quiet about him."

What started out as an interview has turned into something else. This really is a three-way conversation. Among friends.

History Lesson

"I think it was about 11 years ago I first saw Luther play," Brown says. "I knew right then. I knew he was a player from the start."

That was in grade school in Chicago. Brown and Head fast became acquaintances, if not friends. They shared a court from time to time and lived, Brown guesses, no more than "two or three miles apart," but in different neighborhoods. For two kids growing up in one of America's largest cities, that two or three miles might as well have been a million.

"We didn't really hang out, even when we got to high school," Head says. "We pretty much stuck with our own teams. We would see each other and acknowledge that we knew each other, but we weren't friends like we are now."

Head was a year ahead of Brown in high school but even as a senior at Manley didn't

ABOVE: Left to right: Luther Head, Deron Williams and Dee Brown. *Robin Scholz/The News-Gazette*

draw the kind of recruiting attention Brown was getting at Proviso East. Head signed with Illinois. ("The only big school that recruited me at all," he says.) A year later, Brown followed.

That's where the kid from Texas comes into the picture. Brown and Williams became acquainted after the former committed to Bill Self and Illinois. Brown would call Williams on occasion, driving home the message Self and his staff were trying to send: The two players, both heralded point guards, could share the court.

"He was hyper," Williams says. "That was my first impression. I knew his reputation, 'One-Man Fast Break' and all that. He liked to talk."

Williams liked Brown right away. But not so much that he was ready to sign on with Illinois. In fact, the Illini's three-mendous backcourt might never have happened had fate not intervened. Williams was the contingency plan at Kansas, which wanted him only if it hadn't signed Aaron Miles. He was Plan B at North Carolina, too, which told him he'd have a scholarship offer if Raymond Felton chose another school. And the day before Williams was to take his recruiting visit to Georgia Tech—at the time his personal favorite—Jarrett Jack committed to the Jackets.

"Seems like I was destined to end up here," Williams says.

Maybe the stars lined up to bring the trio together. But fate threw a few obstacles in its path, too.

Rising Above it All

First, there was Head's pelvic injury, an ailment that had hindered him his freshman year but threatened to derail his sophomore season altogether. Illinois survived that setback—and Brown and Williams' inexperience—to stay in the Big Ten hunt until the bitter end in 2002-03.

Then things really got interesting. Self left for Kansas. Bruce Weber came on board from Southern Illinois. And Head, finally healthy, spent the first half of 2003-04 battling off-court demons, suspended for two separate incidents. At one point, afraid he was causing too much of a distraction, Head went to Weber and offered to leave the team.

"He didn't tell us he was doing that," Brown says now. "It's hard to imagine. ... It wouldn't have felt right not having him. But it didn't happen."

Head stayed put. And Brown, initially resistant to Weber's way of doing things, started to come around. And down the stretch of last season, Illinois' backcourt stepped to the forefront.

"That's when it started to click," Williams says. "I think we showed a little bit of what we could do."

Consider it a demo tape. Brown, Head and Williams have followed this season with a full-on masterpiece.

It All Comes Together

Head is healthy and happy. Brown and Williams, always impact players, have matured and flourished after a year in Weber's system. The result is perhaps the nation's best set of guards—and perhaps the best in the history of Illinois basketball.

"There's a lot of good guards out there, don't get me wrong," Williams says. "But I think together, we're one of the best backcourts—if not the best."

It's hard to argue with the numbers. Between them, the Illini's starting backcourt averages 43 points, 16.6 assists, 10.4 rebounds and four steals a game.

"They're as good as anybody I've seen this year," ESPN analyst Fran Fraschilla says.

Says Self: "When you have three guys who are unselfish and nobody cares who gets the credit and they can all pass, you're going to have a fun team. That's certainly what they have."

"Unselfish" is the most common superlative thrown around in describing Illinois' trio of guards. Self uses it. Fraschilla uses it. Weber loves to use it. So you ask if that's the key to this backcourt thing, if that's the secret to Illinois' success, and Head thinks for just a second, then shakes his head.

"We just like each other," he says. "I think that's the main thing."

A Like-ly Story

Shaq and Kobe ruined the illusion. They taught us that you can have on-court success in the midst of off-court drama, that a bad soap opera doesn't prevent operatic basketball success. But if Brown, Head and Williams aren't close friends, they're better actors than they are basketball players. And they're awfully good basketball players.

"They really are friends," says Brandon Smith, a team manager who shares an apartment with Head and Brown. "The way you see them play on the court—being cool with each other, sharing with each other—that's how they are in their normal life."

Though they now prefer not to talk publicly about it, Brown and Williams have bonded over being fathers at a young age. Williams lives with his girlfriend and daughter; Brown sees his son, who lives in Chicago, whenever he can.

"Obviously that's something we talk about," Brown says. "It's something we've both been through. I don't want to go into the conversations, but we had 'em. Definitely."

Home life, school and basketball don't leave Williams much free time. What little he has, he says, is spent mostly with his running mates. They watch movies. They eat meals together on the road. But mostly, they compete. At anything. At everything.

"Pie-eatin' contest, whatever you got," Williams says.

They play ping pong (Brown wins). They play poker (Head wins). They play video games (Brown wins again).

"We've got marks on the floor at our house from where those guys are just going at it playing ping pong," Weber says. "They could go play air hockey and they'd compete, and the loser would be really mad."

He wouldn't stay that way. Not for long. Soon, Brown, Head and Williams are laughing with (and at) each other, the way they do when Brown says that he'd make the best coach of the three.

"That's what I'll do when I'm done playing," he says. "I've just seen so many dudes play and I've been through so much, I think I can help people."

"I can't see no coach with braids, though," Williams says. "You're gonna have to cut that hair."

Talking the Talk

On the folding chairs at the Ubben Basketball Complex, Brown and Williams still are arguing, now about the eventual Super Bowl champ.

"He doesn't think Pittsburgh will win it," Williams says. "He's crazy."

"New England," Brown says, ignoring Williams.

Brown often argues, he says, despite knowing he's going to lose. Williams is a confessed "Internet junkie," who backs up his assertions with facts and figures. Brown doesn't bother.

"Like, 60 percent of the time, I'm wrong," Brown says. "I just argue because there ain't nothing else to do."

Sometimes, though, this Illini trio finds itself singing the same tune off the court the way it does at game-time.

"We talk about the future, about things we're going to do together," Head says. "We plan trips and stuff."

A return trip to Las Vegas is in the works, sometime after Brown turns 21 in August. Maybe even later than that. Maybe when all three of Illinois' guards are cashing NBA paychecks.

"These two will be in the league," Brown says. "I don't know about me."

Williams drops his head and laughs, and it's arguing time again.

"He does this all the time—I think it's like a reverse psychology thing," Williams says. "He's definitely going to be in the NBA."

The league can wait, Brown figures. For now, Illinois' three aces want to hit a few more collegiate high notes: another Big Ten title, a trip to the Final Four. Maybe even that elusive national championship. And if you remember them 10, maybe 15 years from now as the best guards in school history, you'd get no argument.

"I would like it if people think that," Williams says. "Right now, you have so much in front of you—trying to win a championship, trying to have a future in the NBA—you don't really have time for that. I think stuff like that will be more special once we're old, when we're all sitting around looking back at this."

GAME 19   JANUARY 20, 2005

Assembly Hall, Champaign, Illinois

LESSON LEARNED FOR ILLINI IN OVERTIME WIN

BY BRETT DAWSON, *News-Gazette Staff Writer*

Bruce Weber screamed and tossed a basketball and called his team names you can't print in the newspaper. He figured maybe that would get the message to sink in. Turns out, he might have needed an assist from Iowa.

Weber's top-ranked Illinois basketball team still is unbeaten—19-0 now after Thursday's 73-68 escape from the Hawkeyes in overtime at the Assembly Hall—but hardly unbeatable, a message Weber tried to drive home at practice Wednesday.

It didn't work then, but Iowa got the Illini's attention.

"You (media) guys and a couple other people were saying we needed to lose a game," Illinois guard Luther Head said after his 25 points bailed out the Illini. "Well, I guess you can take this one as a loss. I know we are."

The standings still show Illinois as unblemished, but the long faces and short answers at Thursday's postgame news conference revealed a team feeling sour midway through one of its sweetest seasons. That happens when you allow a team—even the nation's 23rd-ranked team—to score 40 second-half points, forcing overtime. It happens when you miss easy shots, mishandle easy passes and give up easy baskets against a team that entered the game with two Big Ten losses.

Illinois' motto this season seems to be "Don't Just Win Baby, Win Big." When it doesn't happen, don't expect much joy on Planet Orange.

"We didn't play the way we're capable of playing, and any time your team comes out with a performance like that, you can't be happy," Head said. "... We know we've got work to do."

Weber knew that already. He knew it Wednesday when his team lazed its way through practice, which Weber said is becoming

RIGHT: **Luther Head drives past Iowa defender Adam Haluska in overtime. Head scored a game-high 25 points to go along with six rebounds and six steals.** *Robert K. O'Daniell/The News-Gazette*

Illinois 73 | Iowa 68

a habit the day before a game. That's why he launched a basketball against a backboard and let loose an expletive-laced tirade late Wednesday. He wanted to slap his team back to reality. Iowa handled that for him and almost ended Illinois' perfect season and run at No. 1 in the process.

Iowa made Illinois do things it never does. The Illini fumbled (19 turnovers) and bumbled (32.8 percent shooting) and stumbled most of the night, despite never trailing after the game's opening minutes. But while Illinois never lost its lead, it looked a little like a team that's lost some of its edge.

"We were so much ahead of everyone early because of our veteran group," Weber said. "We were hungry, we guarded, people weren't ready (with their) transition defense, our offense was clicking. Now, people are catching up to us, and are we going to make a move?"

The only move they made Thursday was a rare step backward. Dee Brown and Deron Williams combined for 16 points on 5-of-14 shooting. Illinois' big men were even worse. Roger Powell Jr. and James Augustine shot a combined 3 of 21, Powell 2 of 15.

"He shot the three in front of the bench, I wanted to block it," Weber said of Powell, who was 0 for 3 from three-point range.

While the Illini were firing second-half bricks, Iowa was rock solid. The Hawkeyes made big shots at crunch time, including a Greg Brunner floater with 3.3 seconds to play that sent the game into overtime. They came up short but made Illinois go deep into a meaningful game, a first this season. And though Illinois came through in the end, neither Weber nor his players were particularly pleased with the result.

That, they had in common. The difference is, Weber saw it coming. It's the nature of the game, he said. It doesn't mean his team is lazy or feeling the burden of a perfect start. It means his team can't afford to relax with a target on its back.

"They always say you need failure to learn, but these type of games will make us learn that

	1st	2nd	OT	Total
Iowa (#24)	25	40	3	68
Illinois (#1)	34	31	8	73

Iowa

Player	FGM-A	3FGM-A	FTM-A	O-D REB	A	BLK	S	TP
Haluska	5-12	2-4	0-2	0-6	0	0	2	12
Brunner	6-12	0-1	4-5	3-8	2	2	1	16
Hansen	2-6	0-0	0-0	2-1	0	3	0	4
Horner	3-8	3-6	0-0	0-6	4	0	1	9
Pierce	9-20	2-6	2-4	0-2	5	0	2	22
Thomas	0-1	0-0	0-1	2-3	1	0	0	0
Reed	1-1	1-1	0-0	0-1	1	0	0	3
Henderson	0-0	0-0	0-0	0-0	0	0	1	0
Thompson	1-1	0-0	0-0	0-1	0	0	0	2
Totals	27-61	8-18	6-12	9-29	13	5	7	68
	(44.3%)	(44.4%)	(50.0%)					

Illinois

Player	FGM-A	3FGM-A	FTM-A	O-D REB	A	BLK	S	TP
Head	8-18	4-13	5-7	2-4	0	0	6	25
Powell Jr.	2-15	0-3	5-6	2-5	0	0	0	9
Augustine	1-6	0-0	7-8	4-10	0	2	1	9
Williams	2-5	0-1	0-2	1-5	8	0	2	4
Brown	3-9	1-6	5-6	1-0	2	0	2	12
McBride	0-3	0-3	0-0	1-0	2	0	1	0
Carter	0-0	0-0	0-0	1-1	0	0	0	0
Smith	3-5	0-1	0-0	0-2	0	1	1	6
Ingram	3-6	1-1	1-2	4-0	0	1	2	8
Totals	22-67	6-28	23-31	18-28	12	4	15	73
	(32.8%)	(21.4%)	(74.2%)					

we've got to come out every day and play," Brown said.

Weber might not need to yell to get that point across.

"I'm sure we're going to watch this film over and over again," Head said. "And over and over."

Weber only hopes they're paying attention through repeated viewings. He'd rather not repeat his Wednesday tantrum any time soon.

"Sometimes you run out of things to say," Weber said. "It becomes rhetoric and it's just 'Oh, what is Coach saying now?' Now, if they don't learn a lesson it's going to cost us. We got lucky this time, and it might cost us next time."

RIGHT: James Augustine brings down one of his 14 rebounds against the Hawkeyes. *Robert K. O'Daniell/The News-Gazette*

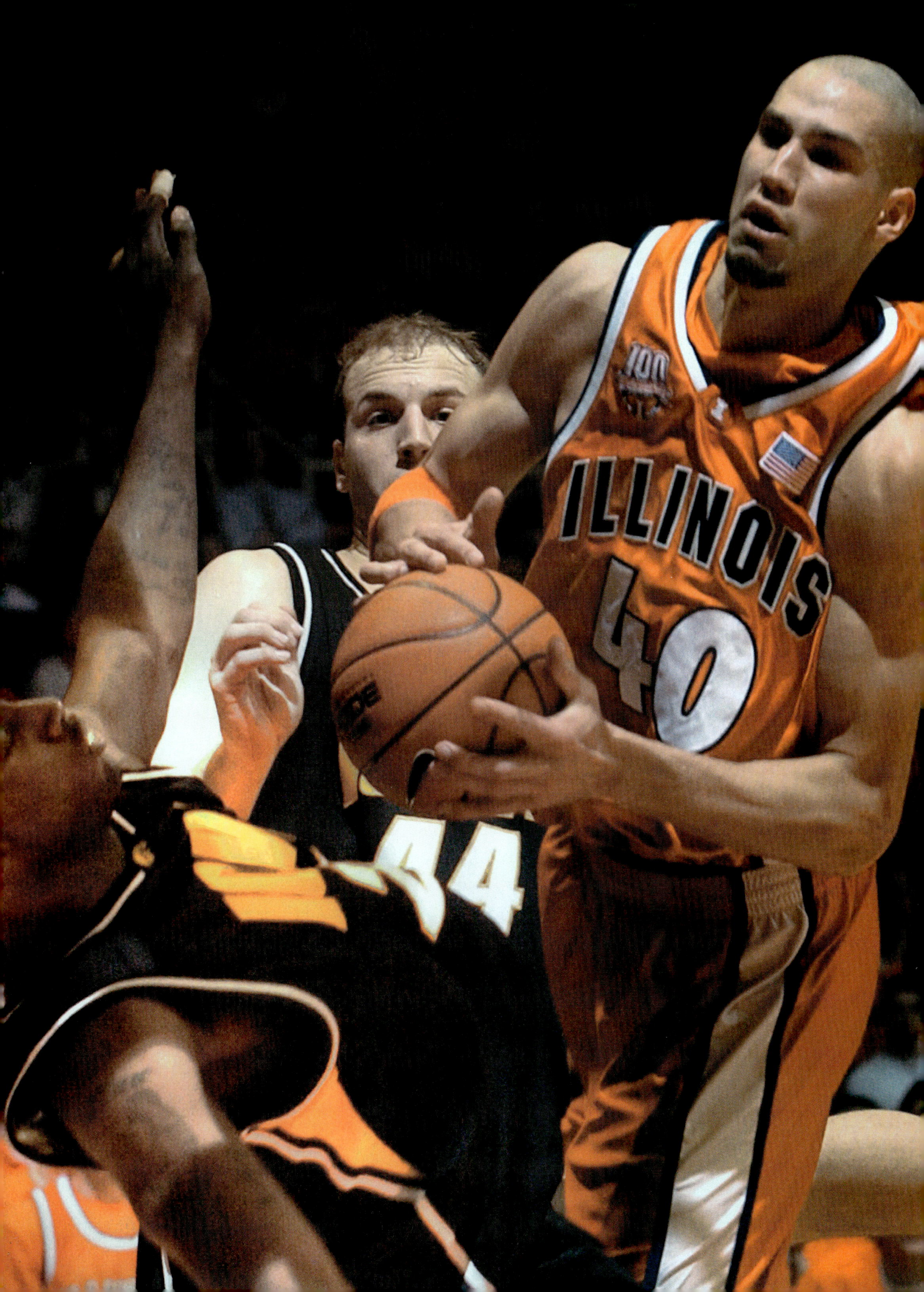
ILLINOIS
40
44

GAME 20   JANUARY 25, 2005

Kohl Center, Madison, Wisconsin

B-E-L-I-E-V-E

BY BRETT DAWSON, *News-Gazette Staff Writer*

You've learned, on the rare occasions when things tightened up on Illinois, that this group of Illini have chilly enough stuff running through their veins. Today, after Illinois' 75-65 win at Wisconsin, you know a little more. The Illini aren't just cool. They're Kohl-blooded.

"I truly believe right now that this team is something special," forward Roger Powell Jr. said after Illinois snapped the Badgers' NCAA-best 38-game homecourt winning streak at the Kohl Center. "God has blessed this team."

Maybe it's not divine intervention, but Illinois certainly looked kissed by fate Tuesday night. Down eight points midway through the second half and playing in a snakepit venue that's been the most magical in college basketball over the past three years, the Illini rallied. And they did it not just behind their stars, but behind key buckets from reserves like Rich McBride and Jack Ingram, a one-two punch from behind the three-point line.

"We've had a lot of great wins—Gonzaga and Wake (Forest)," Illini guard Deron Williams said. "But with the streak they had and the history of the building, (this win) is probably at the top right now."

It's easy to see why. Wisconsin (13-4, 4-2 Big Ten) did what it had done so often during its homecourt winning streak, using a sizzling second-half stretch in which it made 12 of 14 shots to turn a deficit into an eight-point lead. In years past, Illinois (20-0, 6-0) might have wilted like the rest of the Badgers' victims. And for a moment, the Illini's blood boiled. Bruce Weber called a timeout, and his players were at each other's throats.

But not for long.

Turns out, the Illini are cool customers. Even at Kohl. After those heated timeouts, the Illini warmed up. McBride sank an open three to close the gap to five. And minutes later, Ingram buried two three-pointers. The first, with 8:18 to play, tied the score at 58; the second gave the Illini a 61-58 lead.

"I looked up at one point, and I was like, 'Wow, eight points,'" Illinois guard Dee Brown said. "But when you think about it, that's three possessions. When you're a freshman, you don't get that. Now we know: Score a basket, get a stop, score another basket, it's four points. It's not a big deal."

For Illinois, though, Wisconsin's homecourt winning streak—the longest in the Big Ten since the Badgers snapped a 53-gamer at Michigan State three years ago—was a very big deal. Illinois went so far as to root for Wisconsin to rally against Michigan State 10 days ago, when it looked as though the Spartans might end the run at 37.

RIGHT: James Augustine throws down a dunk with authority. Augustine collected 14 points, eight rebounds and two blocks in the game. *AP/WWP*

Illinois 75 | Wisconsin 65

"They truly wanted to come up here and break the streak," Weber said. "I didn't make it a goal, but I think they did in their minds."

The Illini lost a heartbreaker two years ago in Madison, when Devin Harris sank a free throw and Illinois' Big Ten title hopes in the closing seconds. They were blown out a year ago in what proved to be last season's rock-bottom game.

"Early on," Williams said, "we circled this as a game we wanted to do well in when it came up."

And when Illinois has circled an opponent this season, it has done so like a vulture.

"They love big games, they love the limelight," Weber said. "They rise to the occasion."

Wisconsin's was college basketball's most-talked-about streak, but with the win, the Illini continued a series of spectacular spurts of their own. Illinois won its 16th straight regular season conference game (the second-best stretch in school history), its ninth straight conference road game and its 10th consecutive road game overall. That streak of Illinois' is alive and well and looking almost unbreakable.

"We knew we were a good team … ," Brown said. "But as we continue to play, we're starting to get an understanding of how special we can be."

The game began with Weber scrawling a simple message across the dry-erase board in the Illinois locker room: "Believe." It ended with little reason to doubt the Illini.

Almost an hour after the game, after Weber shook more than his share of hands, he shook his head. Box score in hand, he reflected for a moment on what his collection of cool customers accomplished.

"No one's come in here and won for three years," Weber said. "There's no doubt, we've got some kids in that locker room who believe."

	1st	2nd	Total
Illinois (#1)	35	40	75
Wisconsin (#19)	33	32	65

Illinois

Player	FGM-A	3FGM-A	FTM-A	O-D REB	A	BLK	S	TP
Augustine	5-6	0-0	4-4	3-5	2	2	1	14
Powell Jr.	5-7	1-1	0-0	1-2	0	0	0	11
Head	5-10	2-4	6-6	0-2	4	0	1	18
Williams	5-13	0-1	3-4	1-5	6	0	0	13
Brown	2-9	2-5	2-4	0-2	5	0	4	8
McBride	1-2	1-2	0-0	0-0	0	0	1	3
Smith	0-3	0-0	0-0	0-3	0	0	0	0
Ingram	2-4	2-2	2-2	1-5	0	2	2	8
Totals	25-54	8-15	17-20	7-26	17	4	9	75
	(46.3%)	(53.3%)	(85.0%)					

Wisconsin

Player	FGM-A	3FGM-A	FTM-A	O-D REB	A	BLK	S	TP
Tucker	7-10	2-4	0-1	3-5	1	0	0	16
Wilkinson	5-9	0-1	3-4	1-4	1	1	2	13
Chambliss	5-10	4-7	0-0	0-2	4	0	0	14
Hanson	2-8	1-3	1-3	1-2	2	0	2	6
Taylor	3-7	0-3	1-2	0-2	1	1	0	7
Nixon	3-6	3-6	0-0	0-1	3	1	0	9
Morley	0-0	0-0	0-2	0-4	2	0	0	0
Helmigk	0-2	0-0	0-0	2-1	0	0	0	0
Flowers	0-2	0-0	0-0	1-1	0	0	0	0
Totals	25-54	10-24	5-12	8-22	14	3	4	65
	(46.3%)	(41.7%)	(41.7%)					

RIGHT: Jack Ingram came up big off the bench for the Illini, nailing two clutch three-pointers, grabbing six boards, and picking up two steals. *David Stluka/Getty Images*

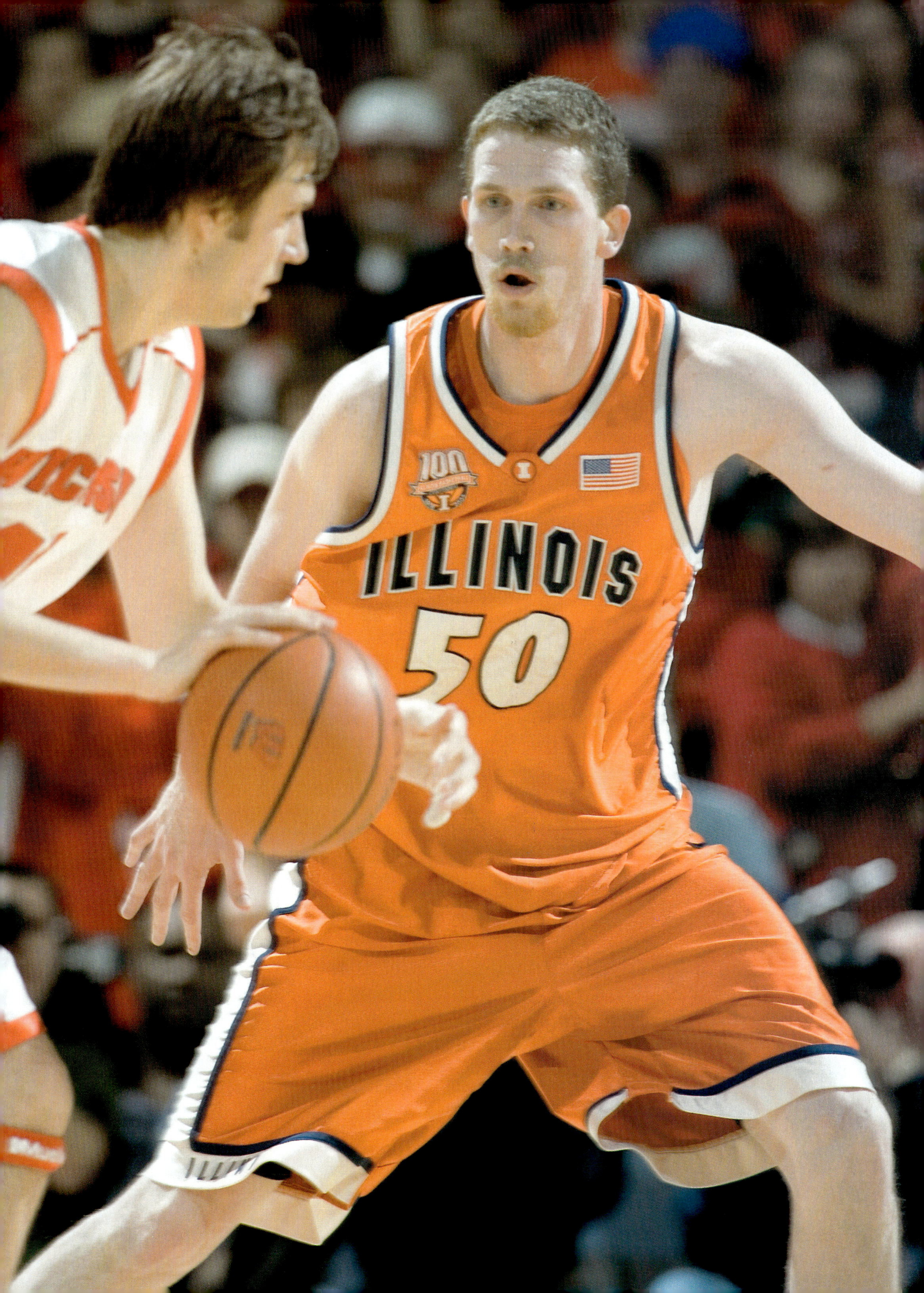
ILLINOIS
50

SMELL THE ROSES

BY LOREN TATE, *News-Gazette Columnist*

January 25, 2005

Sometimes skill isn't enough. Sometimes it boils down to courage ... poise ... discipline. And that's how Illinois severed the nation's longest homecourt winning streak Tuesday night at Wisconsin.

Tuesday's 20th consecutive victory, 75-65 against the Badgers, was unlike any other contest this season. The carnival required 217 media credentials and attracted 18 television stations. A few stragglers from Orange Nation, blessed with bank accounts capable of taking a $300 to $500 hit (for each ticket), were spotted around the Kohl Center. But they were outnumbered by 17,000 deep-throated partisans in a sea of red. It marked the first time all season the top-ranked Illini didn't have extensive vocal support.

And for the first time, the Illini received what could have been a knockout punch in the second half. Lockport's Alando Tucker went berserk with six straight bull's-eyes directly after the break, and the Badgers could smell victory up 56-48.

"They were picking us apart," Illini coach Bruce Weber said. "They had relied on three-pointers in the first half (7 of 13), but they decided to go inside in the second half. We couldn't stop them."

But Wisconsin coach Bo Ryan felt the need to rest star center Mike Wilkinson and Tucker at the same time. Just that quickly, the Illini defense took a bite out of the hosts, who failed on three straight possessions while Illinois climbed back in on Rich McBride's only three-pointer in the last three games and two free throws each by Deron Williams and Luther Head.

In a flash, it was a tossup game again with more than eight minutes to go. And big sub Jack Ingram, who had turned down some earlier looks from the perimeter, drained two straight treys to ignite a 20-7 run in the last eight minutes to seal the deal for the Illini.

Enjoy This One

What we're watching is one of the most remarkable runs in Big Ten history: 16 consecutive Big Ten triumphs and 34 wins in the last 36 games overall.

"Down the stretch, I thought Deron made some great passes," Weber said. "We have guards who can make plays. Wisconsin had a long streak going, and they may have panicked some toward the end. We stopped them on seven of eight possessions when it counted.

"This was a great moment, the most exciting of the year. This is all part of our journey, and we need to smell the roses and keep having fun. These guys enjoy the limelight and the crowd. They rise to the occasion and play their best in the biggest games. They are proud of what they accomplished."

ABOVE: Bruce Weber is congratulated by Illini fans as he leaves the court after Illinois snapped Wisconsin's homecourt winning streak. *AP/WWP*

GAME 21   JANUARY 29, 2005

Assembly Hall, Champaign, Illinois

CURRENT ILLINI KEEP FORMER ILLINI SMILING

BY BRETT DAWSON, *News-Gazette Staff Writer*

All week long, people asked Bruce Weber how he'd keep his team from being distracted as Illinois celebrated its 100th basketball anniversary. Quietly, Weber worried about just the opposite.

"I told the kids, 'We don't want to be a distraction for the weekend,'" Weber said. "We wanted to come in and take care of business so everybody has a great feel for the weekend, the celebration."

Mission accomplished. With an 89-66 rout of Minnesota, top-ranked Illinois (21-0, 7-0 Big Ten) made this a happy birthday celebration. Deron Williams sank jumpers. Roger Powell Jr. went to work inside. And when Dee Brown dropped a fast-break pass to Luther Head for a halftime-buzzer-beating dunk, even Kendall Gill had to stand and applaud.

"We wanted to come out and put on a show," said Williams, who finished with 18 points, five assists and four three-pointers. "We always want to get the job done for us, but this was a special night. The people in the crowd, we wanted to get it done for them, too."

Still, it might've been hard for the 16,694 in attendance at the Assembly Hall to focus much on the past. Not when the present—and future—looks so bright. Illinois is riding its longest in-season winning streak of all time and the longest run at No. 1—Monday will make nine straight weeks—since Connecticut went 10 polls in a row in 1998-1999.

You want history? The Illini are making it right in front of you.

"You couldn't have a better story," Weber said. "All these guys coming back, and we're 21-0."

Weber wondered at times this week what might happen if his team was 20-1 by the end of Saturday, what kind of rain the current Illini would have put on the weekend's parade had Minnesota pulled the upset. He needn't have worried. Like they have all season, the Illini put aside potential distractions, jumping to a 29-12

RIGHT: Former Illini coach Lou Henson meets with the press on game day as part of Illinois' centennial celebration. *John Dixon/The News-Gazette*

Illinois 89 | Minnesota 66

lead and never giving Minnesota a chance to catch its breath.

The Illini in the crowd were all smiles. The ones on the court were happy to see it.

"Kendall Gill, I used to see him in the NBA all the time," said Powell, who scored a season-high 21 points. "Kenny Battle, all those guys. It felt great to win the game like that and compete at the level we did today. I think we showed them a good time."

And that, almost as much as beating the Gophers, was the point. Weber stressed to his team that while the weekend was about the former Illini, the game was all about the current ones. He told them the goal should be to win and improve and stay in the driver's seat for the Big Ten title.

But there was no way he could spin this one into just another game. So he didn't try. He showed his players a clip of Illinois hoops highlights that Weber said, "made your heart pound a little bit," and he stressed their place in the Illini basketball legacy.

"I think they feel special to be a part of this," Weber said. "They saw some of the former guys, and they wanted to perform well, and I think they did."

Weber smiled when asked if Tom Izzo might provide tickets for the Illini's All-Century team so they can watch Tuesday's Illinois-Michigan State tilt in East Lansing, Michigan.

"I don't think they'll have tickets for anybody," he said.

Probably not. The Breslin Center will be packed and the Izzone foaming at the mouth by the time Illinois gets to Michigan State for what could be the most important game in the Big Ten championship chase.

"It's gonna be crazy," Williams said. "The Izzone, they're always pumped up."

For all its tricks, though, the Michigan State student section will have a hard time rattling these Illini. Nothing else has. Not Wisconsin's 38-game homecourt winning streak. Not a gut-check game at home against Iowa. And certainly not a host of former players, coaches and managers sitting courtside at the Assembly Hall.

"All year they've surprised me," Weber said. "Even last year, down the stretch we had to win every game to win the (Big Ten) title outright, and they kept getting enough energy and staying focused. You've got to be pleased with them, the leadership.

"They enjoy the limelight, and yet when it comes time to play and practice, they really get focused."

	1st	2nd	Total
Minnesota	26	40	66
Illinois (#1)	47	42	89

Minnesota

Player	FGM-A	3FGM-A	FTM-A	O-D REB	A	BLK	S	TP
Stamper	2-6	0-0	3-4	1-1	2	0	0	7
Lawson	1-4	0-3	0-0	2-2	2	0	0	2
Hagen	4-6	0-0	2-3	2-4	0	1	1	10
Robinson	1-6	1-4	0-0	0-1	1	0	0	3
Grier	5-17	0-0	7-10	4-4	0	0	2	17
Coleman	5-12	1-4	0-0	3-1	1	0	0	11
Tucker	4-7	2-2	2-2	1-1	4	0	1	12
Tollackson	2-4	0-0	0-0	2-1	0	0	0	4
Webb	0-1	0-1	0-0	0-0	0	0	0	0
Saunders	0-0	0-0	0-0	0-0	0	0	0	0
Nuness	0-0	0-0	0-0	0-0	1	0	0	0
Totals	24-63 (38.1%)	4-14 (28.6%)	14-19 (73.7%)	16-15	11	1	4	66

Illinois

Player	FGM-A	3FGM-A	FTM-A	O-D REB	A	BLK	S	TP
Head	4-11	2-8	0-0	0-2	3	0	0	10
Powell Jr.	8-12	2-3	3-4	2-1	0	0	0	21
Augustine	5-6	0-0	5-6	2-5	1	3	2	15
Williams	7-10	4-5	0-0	1-4	6	0	2	18
Brown	2-6	1-4	2-2	0-4	6	0	3	7
McBride	1-3	1-1	0-0	2-2	0	0	1	3
Carter	1-2	0-1	0-1	0-1	0	1	0	2
Smith	0-3	0-0	0-0	0-4	3	1	0	0
Ingram	3-4	0-0	2-2	3-1	2	0	0	8
Pruitt	2-2	0-0	1-2	1-0	0	0	0	5
Nkemdi	0-0	0-0	0-0	0-0	0	0	0	0
Totals	33-59 (55.9%)	10-22 (45.5%)	13-17 (76.5%)	11-26	21	5	8	89

RIGHT: Roger Powell Jr. scored 21 points on 8-of-12 shooting in the Illini's 89-66 rout of Minnesota. *John Dixon/The News-Gazette*

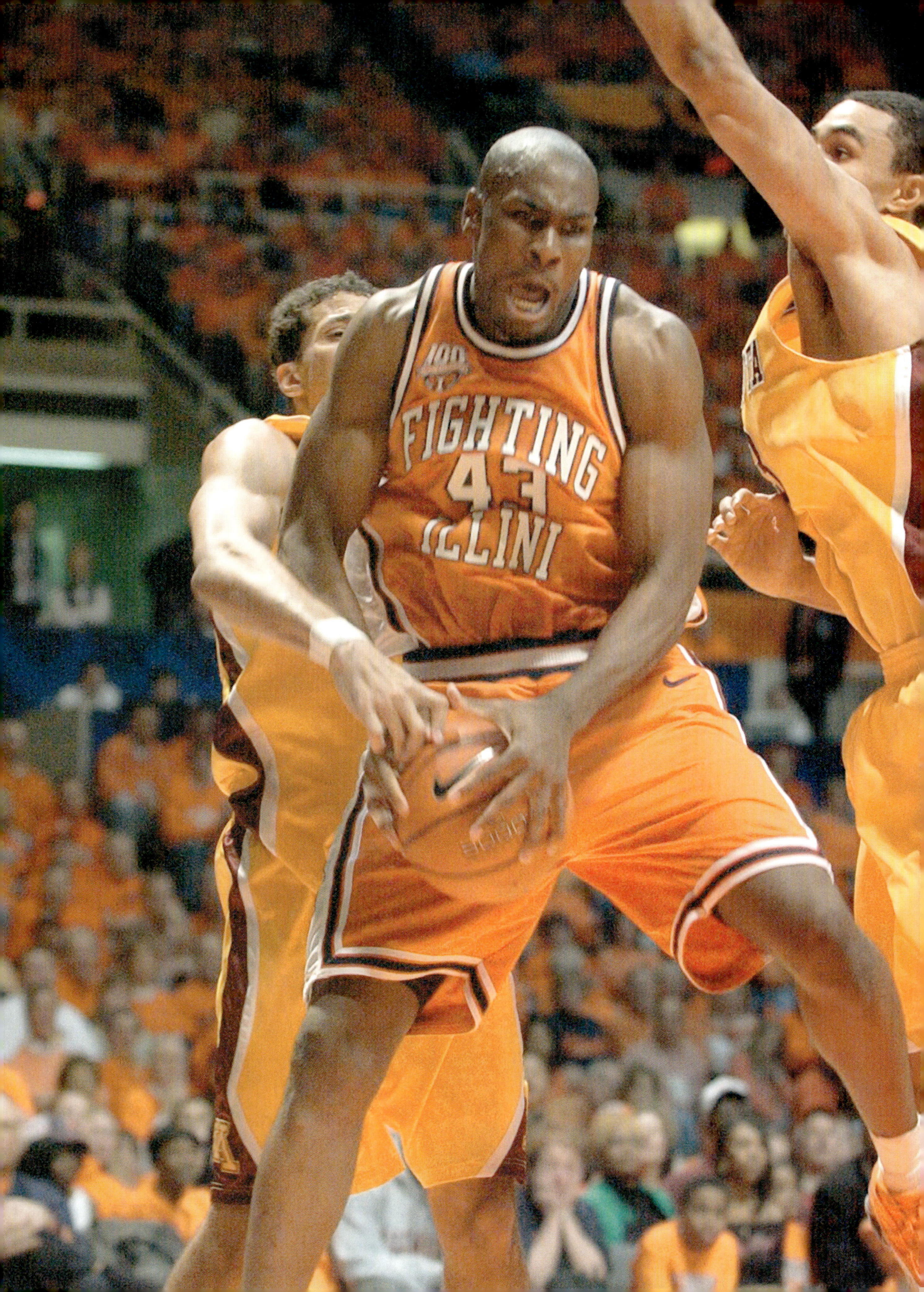
FIGHTING
43
ILLINI

Beyond X's and O's

Old School Meets New School

BY BOB ASSMUSSEN and TONY BLEILL, *News-Gazette Staff Writers*

January 29, 2005

The most popular coach in school history was courtside. So were many of the best living players. And a whole bunch of their fans.

The Illinois centennial celebration had the former players wanting to come back. Sooner rather than later.

"Thanks for the invitation," said former Illini and basketball Hall of Famer Jerry Colangelo, speaking for the 350 ex-players, coaches and support personnel. "I just don't want you to wait another 100 years to do it again, Ron."

That would be Illinois athletic director Ron Guenther, who spent an hour Saturday afternoon happily shaking hands and passing out plaques to the Illini stars. With most of the 16,694 from the Illinois-Minnesota game remaining in their seats for the hour-long ceremony, Guenther recounted the program's success: 16 Big Ten titles, 24 NCAA tournament appearances, four Final Fours, etc.

Saturday's festivities started in the morning with a three-point contest (Lucas Johnson was the stunned winner) and alumni game at Huff Hall. There was an early-afternoon news conference with former Illinois coaches Lou Henson, Gene Bartow and Harv Schmidt. The room was jammed wall to wall with reporters, and Henson kept them entertained with a string of one-liners.

The loudest ovation of the day came at halftime, when Henson was introduced. Seated courtside the entire game, the recovering cancer patient greeted a string of wellwishers. Former Illini Kendall Gill sat with Henson and his wife, Mary.

"It was great to see him in good health and good spirits," Gill said.

The Illini won to extend their school-record start to 21-0.

"Great timing," said Eddie Johnson, an Illini star from 1978 to '81. "I told (organizer) Rod Cardinal, 'You need a bonus, don't you?' You couldn't have written it any better."

Cardinal, the team's director of basketball operations, is responsible for many things, but he can't take credit for the serendipity that has washed across the Illini basketball landscape this season.

Bruce Douglas, a standout guard from 1983 to '86, has an idea how it happened.

"I really believe this is a divine appointment that we have in history, where you bring back players from 100 years of basketball at a time that's the best in history," Douglas said. "You're off to the best start ever. We could not have written a script like that. Only God could orchestrate those kinds of things."

Dozens of players marked the start of weekend festivities by visiting the Rebounders Club luncheon on Friday. The most cherished guest:

ABOVE: Former Illini stars Kenny Battle (left) and Eddie Johnson take time to sign autographs for fan Austin Gernant, 10, of Galesburg, Illinois. The centennial festivities brought a unique opportunity for former players to reconnect to the university, the basketball team and its fans. *Heather Coit/The News-Gazette*

Henson, who returned Thursday via private plane despite recent health problems. Henson's right leg is partially paralyzed after a bout with viral encephalitis, necessitating the use of a wheelchair.

"It was great seeing him," said Kenny Battle, a member of the Illini's 1989 Final Four team. "He wanted to get up, but I wouldn't let him up. He said, 'Kenny, I'm getting up.' You can't keep a man down whose willpower is that strong."

In late afternoon, the group trickled into the Assembly Hall to watch the current team's workout. Afterward, coach Bruce Weber introduced the players to the assembled group.

"There's an aura around here," said Irv Bemoras, who played on the 1952 team that reached the Final Four. "Looking at this current team and how they play, you think, 'Did we do that?'"

Colangelo said the current Illini's unselfishness is their distinguishing trait.

"In a day and age when that isn't so apparent anymore, this team has that characteristic," he said. "Quite honestly, being in the business my whole life, athletes are bigger, stronger, more talented (today). But many of today's young players don't grasp a real knowledge of the game. I think this group has a good feel for the game."

Players had ample chances to catch up with their former teammates during the weekend.

"This is what life really is," Douglas said. "It's about relationships that you develop. At some point in life, you get to rekindle them, and you find out how special they were by what you built when you were together."

The oldest player on hand: Colin Handlon, who graduated in 1940. The player who traveled the farthest: Germany's Jens Kujawa, who played in the late 1980s.

"Once (the attendees) got here and saw their friends and teammates, they did exactly what we thought would happen in terms of their reaction," Cardinal said. "They just took over."

All that's left is for the current Illini to add to the history.

"You just feel this is a team of destiny and is going to win the national championship and be undefeated," said Jim Dawson, a star of the mid-1960s. "It's what they deserve."

GAME 22   FEBRUARY 1, 2005

Breslin Center, East Lansing, Michigan

SPARTANS FALL AS ILLINI FLY HIGHER

BY BRETT DAWSON, *News-Gazette Staff Writer*

On paper, this was the one. On paper, Michigan State caused matchup problems for No. 1 Illinois. On paper, the Breslin Center was the last great roadblock between Illinois and a Big Ten title run—and a perfect season.

Illinois (22-0, 8-0 Big Ten) shredded that paper—and the 12th-ranked Spartans—on Tuesday, cruising past Michigan State 81-68 in what was supposed to be its toughest test yet.

"I can see where you would think that," said Illini guard Deron Williams, who scored 14 points and dished out five assists. "Just because this is a tough place to play, Michigan State (has) athleticism. It's tough to compete with those guys, and they have a great coach. But I don't think we were ready to accept that. We never thought that way."

And no wonder. Nobody's beaten Illinois this season. Hardly anybody has come close. But the Illini's confidence springs less from what's come so far as from what they think is coming.

Here's a scary thought for the Big Ten, and maybe for the nation: Illinois is (gulp) getting better.

"Every single day," Williams said.

Toughened by a gut-check at Wisconsin, Illinois came north this week certain it would leave Michigan State with a win. When that win came, there were high-fives and chest bumps, but hardly the wild celebration that followed last week's similarly impressive win against the Badgers in Madison, Wisconsin.

Not that this was some ho-hum win. Michigan State had won 95 of the last 101 regular season games at the Breslin Center. The Spartans entered the game 10-0 at home this season, averaging 85.5 points a game in the friendly confines. But in front of a white-clad crowd and an energized Izzone, Illinois held Michigan State 12 points below its season scor-

---

RIGHT: Luther Head breaks away after stealing the ball from Michigan State's Chris Hill. Head had five steals to go along with 22 points. *AP/WWP*

Illinois 81 | Michigan State 68

ing average while limiting the Spartans to 42.9 percent shooting. In doing so, the Illini left little doubt that they're a better team than the one that struggled to beat Iowa in overtime two weeks ago—and maybe better than the one that beat Wisconsin last week.

"I think they have the ingredients to win a national championship," Michigan State coach Tom Izzo said. "I don't want to put that on their backs because there are so many other things on their backs, but as Bobby Knight once told me about my team after we beat (Indiana), 'You've got a real chance to win it,' and that was the year we won."

Illinois, Izzo said, has some characteristics in common with his 2000 national championship squad, but the Illini have a few traits all their own. Like the way they bury the opposition from behind the arc (they sank 13 three-pointers against the Spartans); or the way they lock up an opponents' ball handlers (12 steals); or the way they make big plays at just the right moments. But, if there's one thing about his team that gets Bruce Weber giddy, it's the improvement it continues to make, even as the number in the win column keeps climbing.

"That's something we've continued to stress: How can you get better?" Weber said. "They don't seem to get complacent. We've told them it's not enough to stay where you are, and they've really bought into that."

That explains Rich McBride using his dribble to set up Nick Smith for a wide-open layup. It explains why James Augustine's confidence has continued to climb and Williams' jump shot has started to fall.

It seemed appropriate, then, to ask the team Tuesday night: "Who's going to beat you guys?" The Illini are winning their games by an average of 18.5 points, their conference games by 14.6 a night. Iowa and Purdue are the only Big Ten opponents to come within single digits of the Illini. Michigan is hurting. Pierre Pierce's future is in doubt at Iowa. And with no remaining games against teams currently ranked in the Top 25, it's reasonable to wonder if improving Illinois might make it through the regular season unscathed.

"We just take it one game at a time," added Dee Brown, who dazzled with his 18 points, if not with that postgame cliche.

Weber is certain of at least two things. His team is very good. And it is getting better.

"They're very focused on improvement," Weber said. "I just hope we can keep it up."

	1st	2nd	Total
Illinois (#1)	41	40	81
Michigan State (#10)	33	35	68

Illinois

Player	FGM-A	3FGM-A	FTM-A	O-D REB	A	BLK	S	TP
Head	8-15	4-9	2-2	0-2	1	0	5	22
Williams	5-8	4-5	0-0	0-1	5	0	0	14
Brown	7-13	3-6	1-2	0-5	2	0	3	18
Augustine	4-4	0-0	3-4	2-3	2	0	4	11
Powell Jr.	2-5	0-2	4-4	2-2	0	0	0	8
McBride	1-1	1-1	0-0	0-0	2	0	0	3
Smith	1-2	0-0	0-0	0-2	0	0	0	2
Ingram	1-3	1-1	0-0	1-2	2	0	0	3
Totals	29-51	13-24	10-12	6-21	14	0	12	81
	(56.9%)	(54.2%)	(83.3%)					

Michigan State

Player	FGM-A	3FGM-A	FTM-A	O-D REB	A	BLK	S	TP
Brown	4-10	0-3	4-4	1-3	2	0	0	12
Hill	2-3	2-3	0-0	1-0	4	0	2	6
Ager	4-8	2-4	0-0	5-3	2	0	0	10
Anderson	5-13	2-4	2-2	2-3	2	0	0	14
Davis	4-10	0-0	4-4	0-4	3	1	3	12
Neitzel	0-2	0-0	0-0	0-0	1	0	0	0
Trannon	2-4	0-0	0-0	1-2	1	0	0	4
Torbert	3-6	1-4	3-3	0-2	2	0	0	10
Bograkos	0-0	0-0	0-0	0-0	1	0	1	0
Naymick	0-0	0-0	0-0	0-1	0	0	0	0
Totals	24-56	7-18	13-13	11-18	18	1	6	68
	(42.9%)	(38.9%)	(100.0%)					

RIGHT: Deron Williams launches a three in the first half. Williams made 4-of-5 three-point attempts in the game, and the team shot 54 percent from beyond the arc. *AP/WWP*

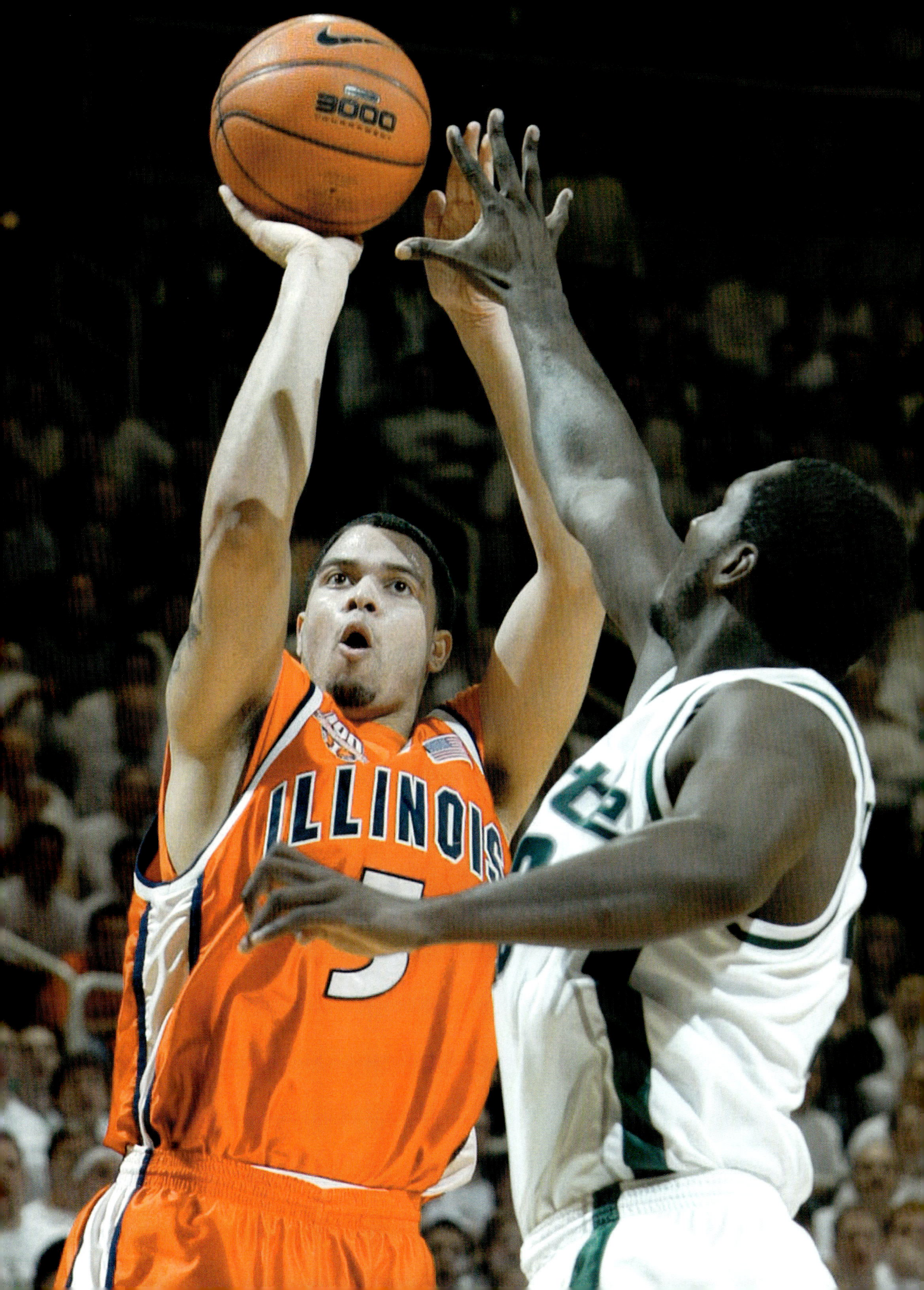
ILLINOIS

SILENCING THE CRITICS

BY LOREN TATE, *News-Gazette Columnist*

February 1, 2005

The Spartan faithful should have been checked for steroids. Nearly 15,000 strong, they turned Breslin Center into a "white-out" madhouse Tuesday night, scorching the ears as they prepared to celebrate the building's 108th consecutive sellout.

Students came with green hair, bare-skinned and painted, or all of the above. In the mix were Superman, Spider-Man and Incredible Hulks. Fairyland released Grumpy and Happy (both went home grumpy), and Frankenstein made the trek. There was the Blue Man Group in green. They hooted and booed everything orange and chastised senior Roger Powell Jr. for smiling at the feverish, lower-level students during warmups. Signs were everywhere, insulting Illinois interlopers while the band enhanced the ear-splitting, mind-altering noise. And from the beginning, from the moment Powell tipped in his miss for a 2-0 lead, Bruce Weber's Illini kept shutting them up, discouraging their ardor, deadening the rampant emotions, spoiling their fun.

Michigan State pulled within 75-68 and had the ball with 2:11 showing after Dee Brown, the flashing UI energizer, drew a technical for elbowing Tim Bograkos after being intentionally fouled from behind. But Michigan State got no closer. Brown exploded for a three-point play at 1:56, and three Illini free throws brought the final tally to 81-68.

That's a 13-point decision in the heart of Spartanland, where the oddsmakers deemed it a virtual tossup, where the media had billed it "the biggest ever" in Breslin's 16 years, where Tom Izzo built a thoroughbred program that is now chasing a 22-0 Illini racehorse.

Silence Is Deadly

"We kept quieting the crowd," Weber said. "Every time we made a run, it deadened them.

"Our guys respond to these challenges. They enjoy the limelight, particularly Dee. He likes big games, and he made some big shots. His personality rubs off.

"Our kids have a huge will to win and great competitive spirit. …Michigan State is a Top 10 team, but we came in here and played with heart. We are smart enough to take what others give us."

The possibilities are now limitless. There is no ceiling. Even though the Illini, at 8-0, are only halfway through the conference season, ESPN's Andy Katz flatly predicted a 30-0 regular season and suggested the Illini will be 32-0 going into the championship game of the Big Ten tournament. Dick Vitale has joined the bandwagon—and even former Notre Dame coach Digger Phelps, who boldly predicted a Michigan State win Tuesday, must recognize the possibilities.

The Illini aren't leaving much room for argument.

RIGHT: Luther Head celebrates the team's 81-68 victory over Michigan State. *AP/WWP*

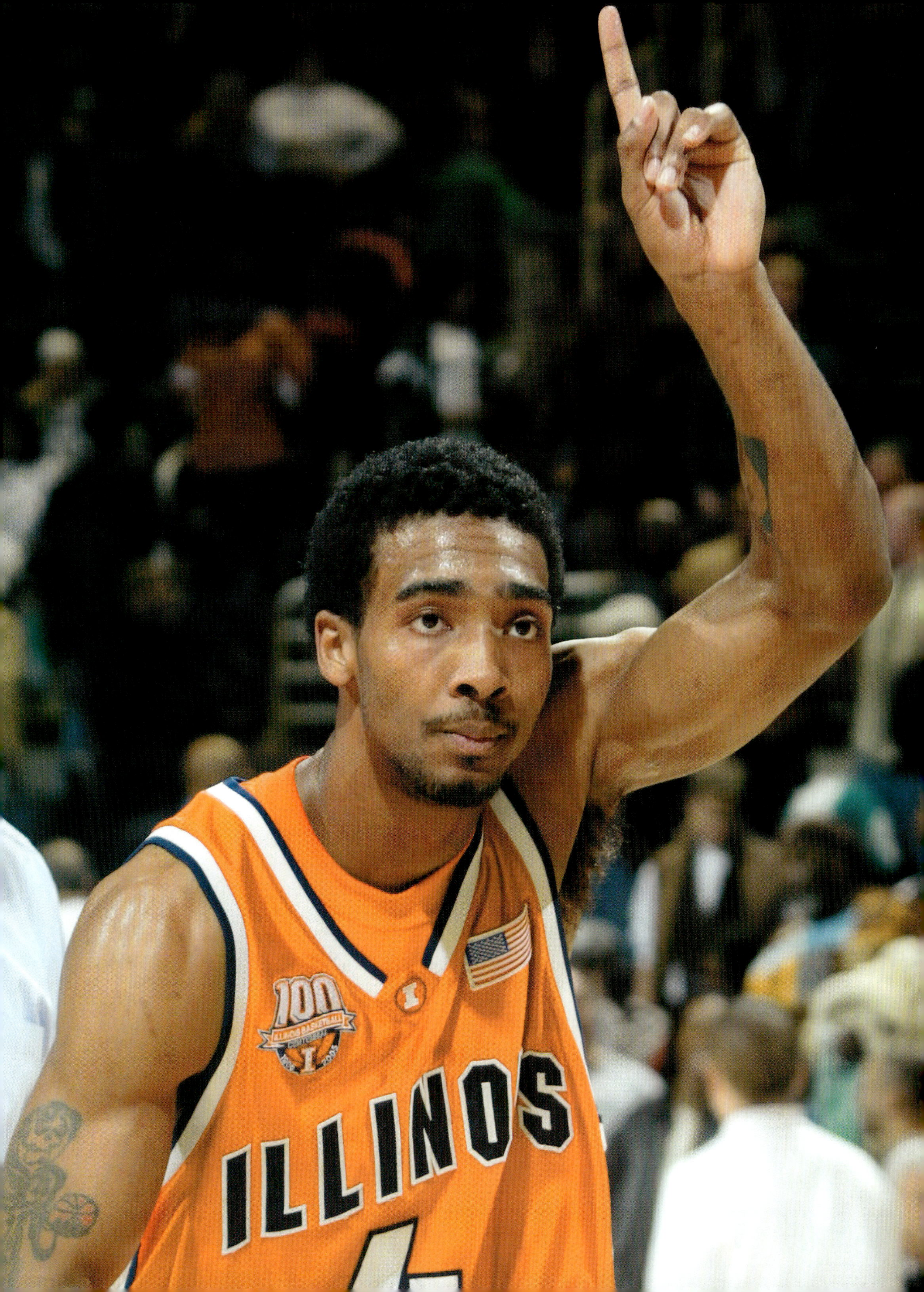
100
ILLINOS

Beyond X's and O's

About Time

BY BRETT DAWSON, *News-Gazette Staff Writer*

February 6, 2005

This is what Bruce Weber means when he says, "Let's do lunch." The Illinois basketball coach bellies up to the clean corner of his cluttered desk upstairs at the Ubben Basketball Complex and picks tomatoes out of a chicken wrap. Satisfied, he takes a bite, then sets the sandwich on its wrapper.

"If we went out to lunch today, we'd have lots of people coming up to us," Weber says. "I can go out in big groups. We try to sit way in the back of the restaurant. People are a little more hesitant to come up to you when it's like that."

Weber isn't complaining. He doesn't mind that he's approached in virtually every social setting, that fans beep their horns and wave or give him the thumbs-up wherever he drives in Champaign-Urbana. ("Seriously, three different people this morning," he says.) Those kinds of encounters in traffic come with the wild ride Weber's on.

Weber is atop the basketball world, the coach of the nation's No. 1 team. That's a considerable climb for a guy who, seven years ago, was wrapping up a 19-year stint as an assistant to Gene Keady and embarking on his head coaching career at age 41.

There isn't time to consider the ascension. There isn't even time to go to a restaurant. Still, once in a while, life reminds Weber of the whirlwind he's riding, and he can't help but shake his head, half-delighted, half-dumbstruck.

"I'm in a high school gym in Kentucky (on a recruiting trip) the other day, and this kid starts yelling out my name," Weber says. "And the coach tells me, 'Two or three of our guys, you're their favorite team.' Can you imagine that? In Kentucky?"

But then, much of what happens these days is outside the realm of Weber's imagination. He spent 18 years at Purdue, watching as other assistants with less reputable resumes and fewer X's and O's tricks up their sleeves got head coaching jobs he couldn't even get interviews for. But in the seven years since he left, his career has taken off at such a dizzying clip, it's all Weber can do to hang on and enjoy the ride.

"It all happens so fast," he says. "One day, you're in the Atlanta airport and some random guy comes up and says 'hello,' and you're like, 'How does that guy know who I am?'"

These days, everybody's getting to know Bruce Weber. Makes you wonder what took so long.

Late Bloomer

If the season ended today, the Illinois coach likely would be the runaway favorite for national coach of the year honors. So, how is it that perhaps the leading candidate for national coach of the year took 19 years to get a head coaching job? It's a fair question. Weber used to ask it a lot.

"The first 10 years, that was when nobody was hiring anybody under 30, 35 years of age," Weber says. "Nobody would've hired me. They'd laugh, like it was some little kid coming looking for a job."

By the time Weber had the experience—and how's this for irony?—he had too much.

ABOVE: Coach Bruce Weber cuts down the net after his Illini defeated Wisconsin to secure the Big Ten tournament championship. *Robert K. O'Daniell/The News-Gazette*

"It's crazy," Weber says, "because (of) my time at Purdue, that length of time really hurt me getting jobs. People would say, 'Why is he still there? There must be something wrong with him.'"

But there was nothing wrong that the knock of opportunity couldn't fix. Weber imagined he'd take over for Keady someday at Purdue, but he was told to prove himself first as a head coach. Southern Illinois gave him the chance. And that's where the wild ride really started.

His Own Man

At Southern, Weber established himself not only as a winner, but as a personality carved from an old-school mold. His formative years in coaching were in the Big Ten's heyday, when Keady and Bob Knight fired verbal salvos on radios and coaches' shows, when Jud Heathcote and Lou Henson were speaking their mind at every turn. Weber thought that's how things were done.

He started the Salukis down a winning path in a hurry. Almost as quickly, he sent a clear message to the Missouri Valley Conference that he was his own man.

"The things he would say," says Doug Elgin, commissioner of the Valley. "I would see him at a press conference, and he would sit up there and say things that I guess a football coach would call bulletin board material, and I think sometimes it hurt him. But that was Bruce."

Right away, Weber proved two things: He was going to win. And he was going to do it his way. The results speak for themselves: Southern Illinois reached two NCAA tournaments in the Weber era, the first culminating in a Sweet 16 run that included a win against Knight and Texas Tech.

And all the while, Weber never changed. Not when MTV came to shoot a documentary on his Salukis. Not when the media attention intensified at the first and second rounds in Chicago. Not a year later, when at an NCAA tournament news conference, he openly discussed his team's displeasure with the amount of media attention given to Missouri Valley rival Creighton. Not even when Ron Guenther called in spring 2003 to discuss the Illinois job.

The rest of the candidates were hush-hush about their involvement. When *The News-Gazette* first contacted Weber in late April 2003, he went on the record saying he wanted the position, even though he knew Guenther preferred that he keep quiet. He got it, and the wild ride picked up speed.

Media Immediacy

Weber may be the same coach he was at Southern, but his life has changed considerably. Every day there's an example of just how far Weber has come. There was the standing ovation his players got at a movie theater earlier this year in Chicago—which still blows Weber's mind—but there are more day-to-day differences, too.

Where he once had to pound the pavement to sell ads for coach's-show sponsorship, Weber now sits back and lets an ad staff deal with that. Where he once slipped into high school gyms with little (or more likely no) fanfare, he now searches for quiet corners from which to observe.

"I went to Peoria the other day, and I could've shaken hands for the length of the game if I'd wanted to," Weber says. "That part is a little tough. When I'm recruiting, I want to watch a kid."

But perhaps the biggest change, and the one Weber most readily discusses, is the media attention he's received at Illinois, particularly during this season's historic start. On Monday, Weber's weekly news conference ran 40 minutes. Afterward, he answered another 20 minutes' worth of questions for print media reporters, then walked to his office for this hourlong one-on-one over lunch (sort of).

But, when you're 22-0, when you're this year's Big Thing in college basketball, not much of your time is your own. Weber is finding that out.

Man About Town

If Weber takes his car in for service, if he goes to pick up his dry-cleaning, if he tries to grab a meal or see a movie in public, there is no chance he'll make it through without talking hoops.

"It's everywhere you go," Weber says. "It's, 'Great season' and 'Way to go against Michigan State.' It's all innocent fan stuff. And then they want to get into next year and recruiting. You get used to it. It's a little hard on your family sometimes, but it's not a big thing."

So Weber obliges. He talks to his orange and blue constituency, engages them as much as he can. Which comes as no surprise to those who know him.

"This is a guy who's not impressed with himself," Elgin says. "The best thing you could say about Bruce is that he forgets his position. Despite all his success, he has never, ever lost perspective on himself or his station in life."

But there are only so many hours in the day—even Weber's day. They all start the same, at about 6:45 a.m., give or take. Weber is early to rise, helping fix breakfast or do the dishes, seeing daughters Emily and Christy—oldest Hannah is a freshman at Purdue—off to school. Then there's the daily dog-walk with wife Megan before he ventures into the office. He's there until 6 p.m. at least, often later. Sometimes he picks up his youngest daughter at an after-school activity before he heads home for dinner, which comes at "7:30 or 8 or 9 or 10," he says.

"Then, after everyone goes to bed, I'll watch film, write, just think basketball," Weber says. "I used to stay up until 2, 2:30 in the morning. Now I'm more of a 1, 1:30 guy."

Except after games. Even this season, with no losses and few close calls, Weber is wired after the horn sounds.

"If we play a game, even if we win, I'm up until 3:30," Weber says. "If I'm lucky. Sometimes later."

At this point, Weber produces a sleek cellphone, checks the caller ID and slips the phone back into the pocket from which it came. It's a ritual he performs countless times during the day. Sometimes it's a congratulatory call from a former player, but even they don't get the kind of time Weber would like to give them. Kent Williams, Weber's star player at Southern Illinois, called a few weeks back. It took Weber 10 days to return his call.

"Every time I thought to call him, it was like midnight," Weber says. "It's awful. I mean, heck, he's the reason I have this job."

There are a few others.

The Ride Continues

Weber has converted the masses to his blunt honesty, his my-way-or-the-highway approach. A 22-0 start has a funny way of doing that. His motion offense is tailor-made for the personnel he has in place. His game plans are virtually flawless.

"I really like that team, and I really like the way he coaches that team," Michigan State coach Tom Izzo says.

So do lots of other people. Looking back, Weber says there's "no doubt" that he values his long road to the top, that coaching outside the spotlight for so long prepared him for the stage he's on now. He admits he doesn't turn heads in a high school gym the way established celebrity coaches like Mike Krzyzewski, Roy Williams and Rick Pitino do. But he turns more this year than last.

"It's not even close," he says.

And that's essential to turning this wild ride into a smooth long-distance one. Professional basketball is about the players. College hoops, with its revolving rosters, is about the coach. So, if Weber's newfound notoriety has its downside, the wild ride has had its perks, too.

Weber wants to keep it going.

"How many jobs are better than this one?" he says. "...I want this to go great, and I want to get more players to keep it going great, and that's all I care about."

RIGHT: Bruce Weber tries to get his team's attention during a game. Attention is the one thing the coach has had little trouble earning this year thanks to Illinois' success on the court. *Robert K. O'Daniell/The News-Gazette*

GAME 29   MARCH 3, 2005

Assembly Hall, Champaign, Illinois

A SPECIAL SENIOR NIGHT

BY BRETT DAWSON, *News-Gazette Staff Writer*

It had been an hour since he'd drained his last three-pointer of the night—a record-tying bomb from 25 feet—and the horde of reporters surrounding Dee Brown had trickled to a scant few. Dressed in an orange Big Ten championship T-shirt, Brown perched on the corner of a table just outside the Assembly Hall press room and considered for a moment how much he'd like to be back in the building one more time this season.

"The Assembly Hall is a great place," Brown said. "It'd be wonderful to come back."

It was Senior Night on Thursday, Illinois romping Purdue 84-50 in its home finale to close the home half of one of the most miraculous Illini basketball seasons ever. But a month from today, Illinois hopes to be playing for a national championship. And if it could pull off that feat, Brown knows the Illini would return to the Hall for one more celebration.

"It'd be unbelievable," said Brown, whose eight three-pointers tied Kevin Turner's single-game school record. "We have to try not to think about that, because thinking about that just gives you the chills. It's gonna be tough, but I think we can do it."

So does his coach. Top-ranked Illinois (29-0, 15-0 Big Ten) already has the Big Ten championship sewn up. It will shoot for a perfect regular season Sunday at Ohio State. But Weber has his eyes on a bigger prize.

"We told them, 'The next big date is April 4,'" Weber said.

That's the night of the national championship game. Weber has designs on being there, and not as a spectator. Why else would he circle the date on his calendar, the way he had circled today's date three weeks ago, when he told his team that's the night it should celebrate a Big Ten title? Why else would his players be sporting T-shirts that read, "The Best Is Yet To Come"?

Thursday was a night to celebrate seniors and toast a title. Sunday might bring perfection. Weber and his team want more.

"I think they realize that we've got a lot more to do," Weber said. "March just started, and we hope it's a long month for us."

March came in like a lion, with a slaughter of Purdue—Brown's seven first-half threes gave the Illini as many points at halftime as the Boilermakers would manage the entire game—

RIGHT: Jack Ingram (left) and teammates hoist the Big Ten trophy during Illinois' postgame celebration of a second consecutive outright league championship. *John Dixon/The News-Gazette*

Illinois 84 | Purdue 50

and Weber hopes his team keeps roaring right into April. Ohio State lies in wait, its best shot at national recognition coming Sunday when an undefeated Illini team comes to Columbus for a game on CBS.

"Two weeks ago they started talking about us and our game and hoping we were undefeated when we came in there," Weber said. "Along the way, they've lost some games, so maybe they should've focused on somebody else."

For the Buckeyes, though, Sunday is the NCAA tournament. For Illinois, it's a chance to make history. Weber couldn't have scripted it this way.

"It is kind of storybook right now," Weber said. "You just kind of hope it keeps going. That's why we told them, 'March 3 has passed, so April 4 is the next big date.' If you're playing that night, it really is a special season."

This is a coach who still can't believe the break he got from Gene Keady 25 years ago, when Keady hired Weber at Western Kentucky.

He's a guy who, on the night he celebrated his second consecutive outright Big Ten title, recounted a time this season when during a recruiting trip, he got out of the private plane he had boarded in Cincinnati to help de-ice the wings.

"I wanted to live," Weber said.

So the coach won't big-time anyone. But his team is as big-time as it gets. One regular season win from perfection and six NCAA tournament wins from its ultimate goal, Illinois took Thursday night to reflect. A post-game highlight video drew smiles and high-fives, and each Illinois player snipped a strip of net from the goal at the south end of the Assembly Hall.

It was a fitting end to a perfect home season.

But in this storybook season, Weber and his team would like to write one more chapter at the Hall.

"We've talked about it a little bit," Weber said. "I hate to even bring it up, but that would be your ultimate goal, to have that special celebration at the end. We'll put some more nets up and cut 'em again."

	1st	2nd	Total
Purdue	26	24	50
Illinois (#1)	50	34	84

Purdue

Player	FGM-A	3FGM-A	FTM-A	O-D REB	A	BLK	S	TP
Ware	6-8	0-0	0-0	2-1	1	1	0	12
Kiefer	4-8	2-3	0-0	2-3	2	2	0	10
Teague	2-15	0-6	0-0	2-4	1	0	2	4
Ford	0-2	0-2	0-0	0-0	1	0	0	0
McKnight	3-15	2-4	0-0	1-5	3	0	2	8
Hartley	0-2	0-1	0-0	1-1	2	0	0	0
Price	2-4	2-3	0-0	1-0	1	0	0	6
Carroll	0-1	0-0	0-0	1-1	0	0	0	0
Liddell	0-1	0-1	0-0	0-1	0	0	0	0
Davis	3-6	0-0	4-4	3-5	0	1	1	10
Totals	20-62	6-20	4-4	14-23	11	4	5	50
	(32.3%)	(30.0%)	(100.0%)					

Illinois

Player	FGM-A	3FGM-A	FTM-A	O-D REB	A	BLK	S	TP
Head	4-10	1-6	2-2	0-5	6	0	2	11
Powell Jr.	1-2	0-1	3-6	0-3	1	0	0	5
Augustine	2-3	0-0	3-3	2-2	1	1	2	7
Williams	7-9	4-6	3-4	0-5	6	0	1	21
Brown	9-12	8-10	1-2	0-1	1	0	0	27
McBride	1-2	1-2	0-0	0-1	4	0	0	3
Carter	1-1	0-0	0-0	1-5	1	0	1	2
Smith	1-3	1-1	1-2	0-2	1	0	0	4
Ingram	1-4	0-1	2-4	1-1	0	0	0	4
Pruitt	0-1	0-0	0-0	0-0	0	0	0	0
Nkemdi	0-3	0-0	0-0	0-1	0	0	0	0
Totals	27-50	15-27	15-23	4-27	21	1	6	84
	(54.0%)	(55.6%)	(65.2%)					

RIGHT: Dee Brown celebrates after his three-point shot went in to conclude play in the first half. Brown scored 27 points and tied a school record with eight three-pointers. *John Dixon/The News-Gazette*

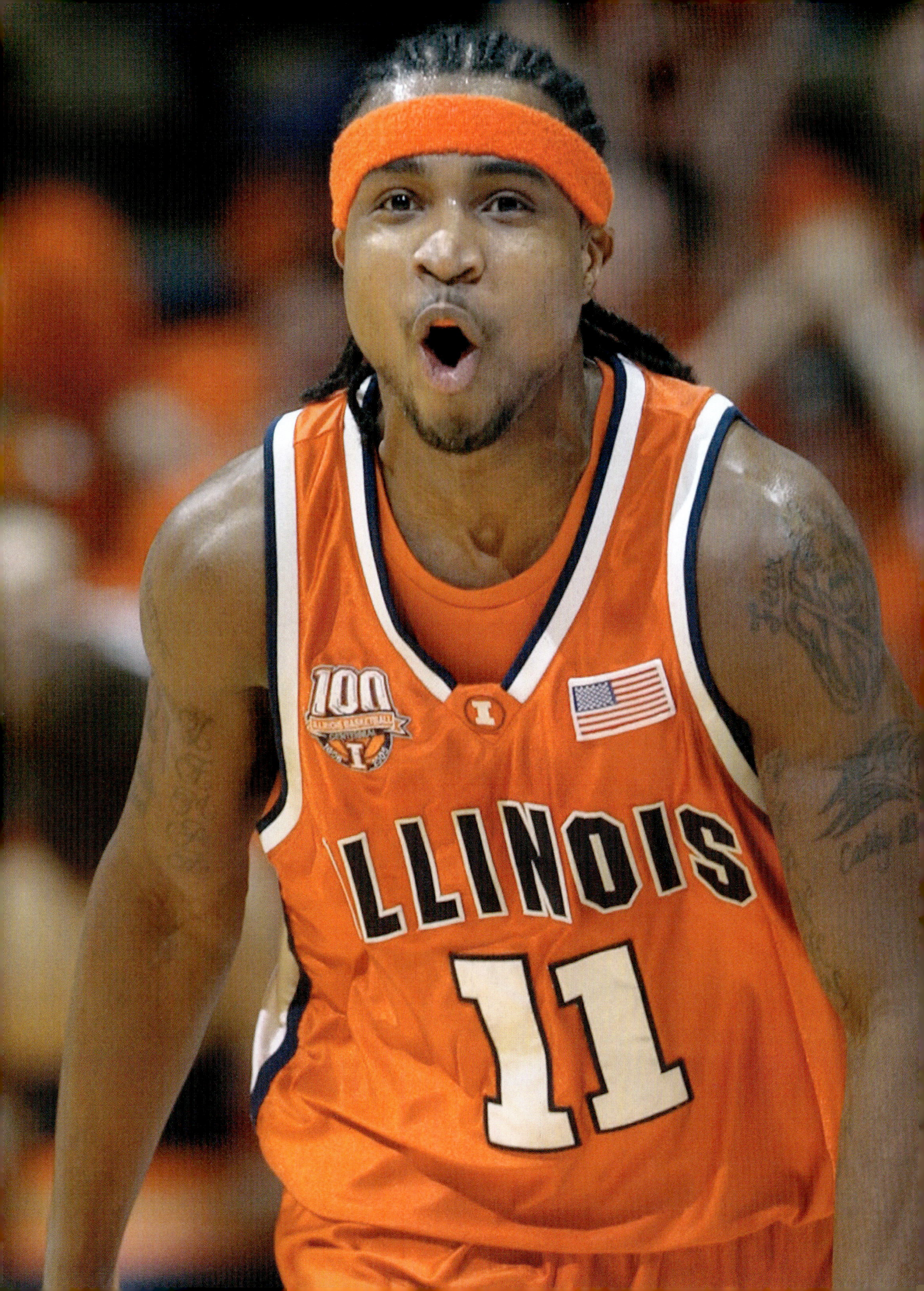
100
ILLINOIS
11

BE SELECTIVE. CHOOSE GREAT TASTE.
Miller Lite has more taste than Bud Light & half the carbs.

Illini Basketball's 100th Year...
- **Outright Big Ten Champs**
- **Conference Tournament Champs**
- **NCAA #1 Seed**
- **Final Four in St. Louis**

Miller. Good call.

Thanks for the Memories!

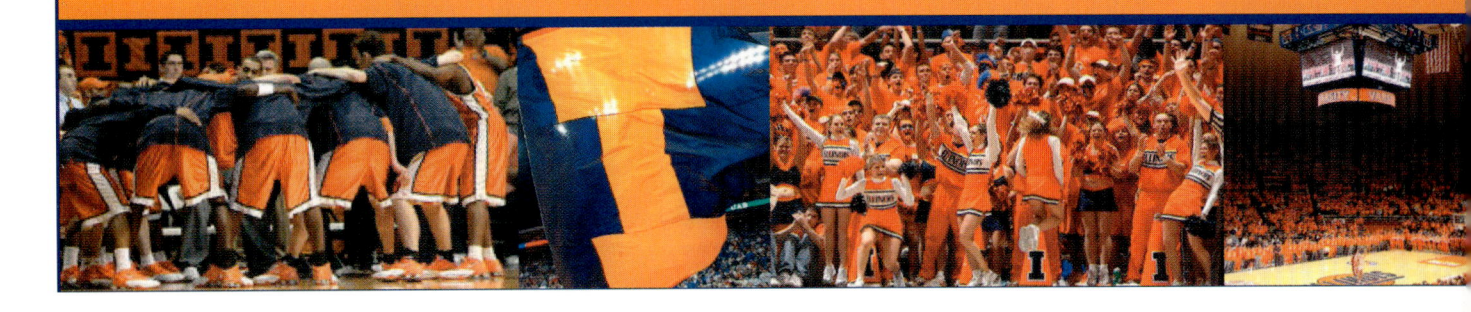

O&B ORANGE & BLUE DISTRIBUTING CO., INC.

© 2005 Ameren Corp.

May every team find the power.

We're proud to salute the Fighting Illini on a tremendous 2004/2005 season.

Ameren
ameren.com

GAME 30 MARCH 6, 2005
Value City Arena, Columbus, Ohio

ILLINI SING THE BLUES IN REGULAR SEASON FINALE

BY BRETT DAWSON, *News-Gazette Staff Writer*

James Augustine strolled out of the Illinois locker room, iPod clipped to his collar, and stopped to meet the press. James Taylor's greatest hits spilled from his earphones. It was that kind of afternoon for the Illini.

"I'd probably be listening to it even if we won," Augustine said.

For 29 games, though, Illinois' season had been set to a more up-tempo soundtrack. On Sunday, Taylor's blue notes were particularly fitting for the Illini. They were playing happier tunes courtside after Matt Sylvester fired and Ohio State ended Illinois' reign with a 65-64 upset that sent shockwaves across college basketball.

Ohio State fans stormed the court. The press swarmed the Illini.

"We finally lost, like y'all wanted us to," Dee Brown said on a brisk walk to the bus, stopping only briefly and answering every reporter's question with, "They just played good basketball."

In doing so, the Buckeyes (19-11, 8-8 Big Ten) wrote a chapter in their hoops history and kept Illinois from etching its name in the record books. They probably still are the heavy favorite for the overall No. 1 seed in the NCAA tournament. But, Sunday's loss dashed Illinois' chances at becoming the first team since Indiana in 1976 to go undefeated en route to the national championship.

"It's disappointing, but it's not the end of the world," Augustine said. "You've got to go into March (and the postseason) thinking differently. If we had gone undefeated and lost in the first round of the NCAA tournament, nobody would think twice about our season. It's how you finish that counts."

If that's true of games as well as seasons, then Sunday's loss is as bad as it gets for Illinois. The Illini led 51-39 with 11:34 to play in the game, but Ohio State outscored Illinois 26-13 down the stretch as the Illini missed shots that always fall and struggled on defense, where

RIGHT: Illinois had no answer for Ohio State's Matt Sylvester, who netted 25 points and the game-winning shot. *AP/WWP*

Ohio State 65 | Illinois 64

they always thrive. Illinois' vaunted guard trio of Brown, Deron Williams and Luther Head was held scoreless over that stretch and finished the game with 27 points on 7-for-27 shooting. And the Illini's pressure defense was nonexistent after halftime—the Buckeyes had eight turnovers in the first half, but none in the second.

On offense, Ohio State turned to Terence Dials and Sylvester, who combined to score 46 points. Sylvester poured in a career-high 25 including a three-pointer with 5.1 seconds to play that provided the game's first—and last—lead change. Roger Powell Jr.'s three-point attempt at the buzzer missed for the Illini, and with that the fans spilled onto the court and the Illini headed for the exits.

"They deserved to celebrate," Powell said.

But this wasn't supposed to be a celebration for the Buckeyes. It was supposed to be a coronation for the Illini, who had played only one game—against Iowa at the Assembly Hall—in which the final possession of regulation mattered.

"We wanted this game," Williams said. "We wanted to go 30-0. That's no surprise. But this just makes us hungrier. … We're going to come to practice on Tuesday and work."

And there's work to do. Ohio State ran to perfection what has long been considered the game plan for beating Illinois. The Buckeyes pressured up on the Illini guards, forced the ball to go inside and hoped their advantage on the interior would pay off. And while Powell finished with 12 points and 11 rebounds, he and Augustine were a combined 8 for 21 from the floor as Illinois shot 38.3 percent overall.

"Whatever you get, you try to use as a motivator," Bruce Weber said. "I just tried to go right at them (in the locker room) and tell them how special they've been and how much they have to celebrate. It really wasn't one of our goals (to go undefeated). Maybe I screwed up. I should've said undefeated (was a goal)."

Weber's goal, he reiterated Sunday afternoon, is to thrive in the postseason. So, Illinois took some time to mourn the passing of an undefeated season, to play a sad song or two. But soon, the Illini said, they'll be back to an upbeat tune.

"Walking off the court, I was really focused on, 'Where do we go from here? How do we get better?'" Powell said. "That's the way you've got to be. You can't live for yesterday. You've got to live for tomorrow, and that's what this team does well."

	1st	2nd	Total
Illinois (#1)	38	26	64
Ohio State	27	38	65

Illinois

Player	FGM-A	3FGM-A	FTM-A	O-D REB	A	BLK	S	TP
Augustine	4-11	0-0	1-3	3-5	0	0	0	9
Powell Jr.	4-10	0-2	4-5	6-5	1	0	0	12
Head	3-9	3-6	3-3	0-7	6	0	1	12
Williams	1-7	0-4	0-0	1-5	3	1	1	2
Brown	3-11	2-6	5-8	0-0	4	0	0	13
McBride	0-0	0-0	0-0	1-0	0	0	0	0
Carter	2-2	0-0	0-0	1-0	0	0	0	4
Smith	2-2	0-0	0-0	0-0	0	0	0	4
Ingram	4-8	0-1	0-0	0-1	0	0	3	8
Totals	23-60	5-19	13-19	13-24	14	1	5	64
	(38.3%)	(26.3%)	(68.4%)					

Ohio State

Player	FGM-A	3FGM-A	FTM-A	O-D REB	A	BLK	S	TP
Sullinger	1-3	0-0	0-0	0-5	1	0	1	2
Harris	0-0	0-0	0-0	0-0	0	0	0	0
Dials	8-13	0-0	5-7	5-3	3	1	1	21
Butler	0-2	0-1	0-0	0-2	0	0	0	0
Foster	3-8	2-5	2-3	0-2	2	1	1	10
Fuss-Cheatham	2-4	0-1	1-2	0-2	2	0	0	5
Stockman	1-6	0-4	0-0	1-3	3	0	0	2
Sylvester	8-17	2-5	7-9	0-5	3	1	0	25
Marinchick	0-0	0-0	0-0	0-0	0	0	0	0
Totals	23-53	4-16	15-21	7-24	14	3	3	65
	(43.4%)	(25.0%)	(71.4%)					

RIGHT: Roger Powell Jr. pulls down one of his 11 rebounds. Powell added 12 points in the losing effort. *AP/WWP*

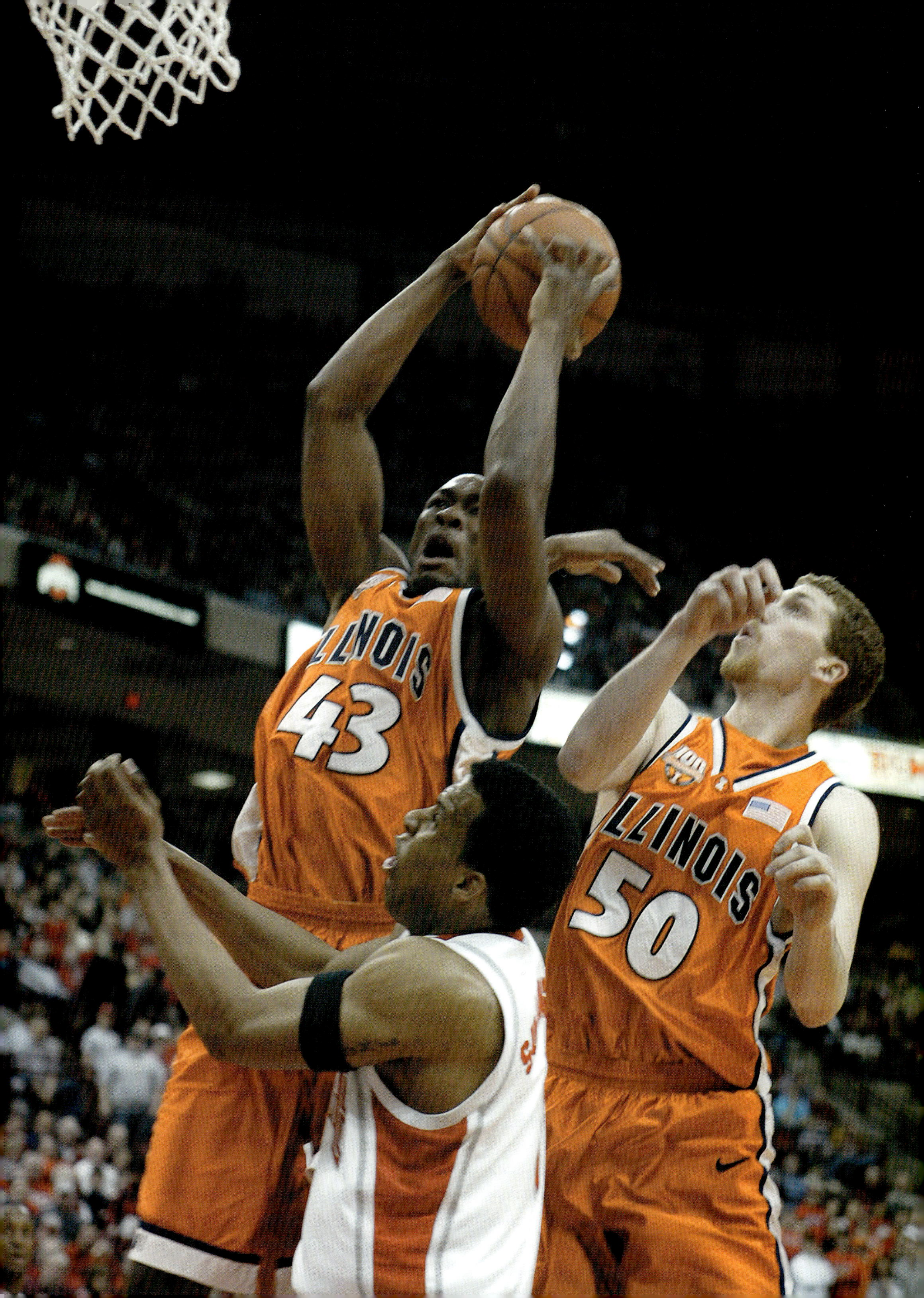
ILLINOIS
43
ILLINOIS
50

BIG TEN TOURNAMENT, QUARTERFINALS   MARCH 11, 2005

United Center, Chicago, Illinois

SLUGGISH ILLINI KNOCK OUT WILDCATS

BY BRETT DAWSON, *News-Gazette Staff Writer*

Maybe it was the early tipoff time. Maybe it was a lingering letdown from the season's first loss. Whatever the case, it took Illinois some time to get started in its Big Ten tournament opener. What many expected to be a start-to-finish clinic against Northwestern instead turned into a sometimes-ragged 68-51 Illini win.

"We were a little bit sluggish in the beginning," Illinois coach Bruce Weber said. "Deron (Williams) did a great job giving us energy."

Illinois didn't do much to wake up the partisan crowd at the United Center with a sluggish start. But by the time Dee Brown lobbed a fast-break pass off the backboard for a Williams layup, the Illini were rolling. It just took awhile to get started.

Not that Illinois isn't movitated as it heads to a second-round game against Minnesota.

"We're playing for a lot, too," said forward James Augustine, who paced the Illini with 15 points and eight rebounds. "We want to prove that we're still a great team, that we haven't lost our mojo or whatever everybody says. (Minnesota is) playing for a lot, but we're playing for a lot, too."

Illinois will be playing with a lot on its mind in Saturday's semifinals. Weber left the United Center immediately after his postgame news conference Friday to meet his mother at Rush University Medical Center, where she was taken after feeling chest pains as she waited to enter the arena Friday morning. Dawn Weber, 81, underwent heart surgery Friday night for a rupture of the descending aorta, and she died in surgery. Weber said he'd coach against the Gophers.

"This has been a great loss to our family," Weber said in a statement released by the university. "My mother has been very influential in my life and career, and that is why I have decided to coach the team (today), because that is what she would have wanted."

After meeting with his staff and players, Weber made the decision to coach today's game.

"Obviously, despite all the great things that have happened to our team this year, a day like today makes you realize the most important things in life, and that is your family," Weber said.

Before he learned of his mother's condition, though, Weber's worries centered primarily on

Illinois 68 | Northwestern 51

his team's sometimes lackluster quarterfinal effort against the Wildcats. Illinois missed 15 free throws against Northwestern (15-16) and had 16 turnovers. And though Weber was pleased with his team's defensive effort—the Wildcats had 19 turnovers and shot 34.5 percent—he wasn't always thrilled with its energy.

"I hoped after a loss they'd have a little more energy," Weber said. "I wish they would play harder, or play with a lot more energy or enthusiasm. I just hope we don't get caught because we think we can turn it on, and all of a sudden we (can't) turn it on. We couldn't finish it at Ohio State."

	1st	2nd	Total
Northwestern	22	29	51
Illinois (#1)	38	30	68

Northwestern

Player	FGM-A	3FGM-A	FTM-A	O-D REB	A	BLK	S	TP
Vukusic	6-14	2-5	1-2	0-4	3	0	1	15
Hachad	7-16	2-5	7-11	2-7	2	1	2	23
Duvancic	2-6	0-0	0-1	1-5	2	0	2	4
Parker	0-3	0-1	1-2	1-1	2	0	2	1
Jenkins	1-5	1-4	0-0	0-4	0	1	1	3
Kennedy	0-1	0-1	0-0	0-0	0	0	0	0
Doyle	1-2	0-0	1-2	2-3	4	0	1	3
Seacat	0-0	0-0	0-0	0-0	0	0	0	0
Scott	1-5	0-3	0-0	0-1	0	0	0	2
Totals	18-52 (34.6%)	5-19 (26.3%)	10-18 (55.6%)	9-27	13	2	9	51

Illinois

Player	FGM-A	3FGM-A	FTM-A	O-D REB	A	BLK	S	TP
Head	5-14	2-8	2-4	1-5	3	1	0	14
Powell Jr.	3-4	0-0	5-9	4-3	0	0	0	11
Augustine	6-8	0-0	3-7	3-5	2	0	2	15
Williams	3-8	1-2	1-3	0-2	8	0	2	8
Brown	2-4	1-3	0-0	0-2	6	0	2	5
McBride	1-5	0-3	3-3	0-1	1	0	1	5
Carter	0-1	0-1	0-2	0-5	0	1	0	0
Smith	3-5	0-1	0-0	1-4	0	1	0	6
Ingram	1-2	0-0	0-0	0-0	0	0	0	2
Pruitt	1-1	0-0	0-1	0-2	0	0	0	2
Nkemdi	0-0	0-0	0-0	0-0	0	0	0	0
Totals	25-52 (48.1%)	4-18 (22.2%)	14-29 (48.3%)	9-31	20	3	7	68

BELOW: Roger Powell Jr., Dee Brown, Deron Williams and James Augustine relax on the bench during the second half of Illinois' 68-51 victory over Northwestern. *Robert K. O'Daniell/The News-Gazette*

BIG TEN TOURNAMENT, SEMIFINALS   MARCH 12, 2005

United Center, Chicago, Illinois

WINNING ONE FOR COACH

BY BRETT DAWSON, *News-Gazette Staff Writer*

James Augustine was the first to reach his coach when the game ended, wrapping a long arm around Bruce Weber's shoulders and smiling as he delivered a message.

"We got one more, Coach," Augustine told Weber moments after Illinois' 64-56 win against Minnesota in Saturday's Big Ten tournament semifinal.

It was hardly a heartfelt message, merely a reminder that with one more win against Wisconsin in the Big Ten Tournament final, the Illini will add a tourney title to the regular season crown they claimed.

Many tears were shed in the hours since Weber's mother, Dawn, died Friday during heart surgery. There were condolences and prayers and a powerful moment of silence before the Illini and Gophers tipped off. And for a little while, at least, Illinois wanted to think about basketball.

"(Weber) is a hard worker, a blue-collar guy who just wants to do his job as best he can," said Illinois forward Jack Ingram, who served as the team's spokesman for its pregame meeting with the coach. "If we could've given him a two-hour break from feeling some of the pain and he could just get lost in the game, that would be a good (thing)."

When he berated referee Zelton Steed, when he implored Dee Brown to pressure the ball, when he called out plays in that trademark booming screech, Weber looked like a man comfortable on the sideline, a man coaching any other game on any other day. But Saturday was hardly that.

When he arrived at the United Center about an hour before tipoff, Weber entered, head down, to dozens of reporters, flashing cameras and six arena security employees who escorted him a short walk. He stopped briefly in a room just down the hall from the Illinois locker room for an interview with ESPN, then proceeded to the locker room, where he met with his team and listened as Ingram spoke on his teammates' behalf.

"I just wanted to really convey our support for him," Ingram said. "He had a tough loss in his family, and we just wanted to thank him for being able to come here and coach us and lead us."

Weber got emotional during that meeting, his players said, and the emotions spilled over

RIGHT: Bruce Weber becomes emotional during a moment of silence for the loss of his mother, Dawn, before the Illini tipoff against Minnesota. *Robert K. O'Daniell/The News-Gazette*

Illinois 64 | Minnesota 56

onto the court. When the crowd of 23,697—a Big Ten tournament record—applauded after a moment of silence, Weber waved to the crowd with tears streaming down his face. In the crowd, an Illinois fan held up a sign that read, "Saddened by your loss, inspired by your courage."

"There's been a lot of tears since 6 o'clock (Friday)," Weber said two hours later at his postgame news conference. "Tears of good things, of all the time we had together. She was a great mom. But at the same time, it is emotional. It gets a little bit of a knot in your stomach."

Weber called the game "no doubt" the most difficult of his coaching career. It was only slightly easier for his players. The Illini fought their way to what the team called an important win, one they wanted for their coach. But it rarely went smoothly. Illinois committed a season-high 23 turnovers and shot 35.7 percent.

"I think we just wanted to win so bad for him we tried to do too much early on," guard Luther Head said. "You could see that we were really struggling and forcing some things. We knew how he felt, and I just think we didn't want to let him down."

They didn't. Not even when Minnesota whittled a 14-point lead to two and came charging at the Illini with all the momentum it could muster. Augustine finished with 11 points and a career-high-tying 14 rebounds, and the Illini stifled Minnesota star Vincent Grier down the stretch to give their coach the victory.

"For Coach Weber to even coach the game, that's big time," said Wisconsin's Alando Tucker, whose game-winning three-point bank shot Saturday against Iowa gave the Badgers a crack at Illinois in today's title game. "But it's big time for those players, too. I know those guys, I know their program, and you could see they started out a little slow (against Minnesota), but they hung in there through all that emotion. That's a tough team."

If that's true, the Illini said, credit the man at the top.

"For him to come out here and coach us today, it shows how strong a person he is,"

	1st	2nd	Total
Minnesota	24	32	56
Illinois (#1)	30	34	64

Minnesota

Player	FGM-A	3FGM-A	FTM-A	O-D REB	A	BLK	S	TP
Coleman	0-2	0-0	0-0	1-1	0	0	0	0
Lawson	2-5	2-4	2-2	3-4	3	0	0	8
Hagen	4-10	0-0	2-2	3-2	1	3	0	10
Robinson	4-9	4-8	0-0	0-3	6	0	2	12
Grier	10-25	0-3	4-8	2-6	3	1	3	24
Stamper	0-2	0-0	0-0	0-1	0	0	0	0
Tucker	1-3	0-2	0-0	1-0	0	0	1	2
Tollackson	0-1	0-0	0-0	0-0	0	0	1	0
Totals	21-57 (36.8%)	6-17 (35.3%)	8-12 (66.7%)	13-20	13	4	7	56

Illinois

Player	FGM-A	3FGM-A	FTM-A	O-D REB	A	BLK	S	TP
Head	5-13	4-9	0-2	1-5	4	2	1	14
Powell Jr.	3-5	0-0	4-5	6-2	0	1	0	10
Augustine	3-6	0-0	5-7	6-8	1	0	1	11
Williams	4-9	1-2	3-3	0-5	5	0	2	12
Brown	2-12	2-9	4-6	2-2	0	0	2	10
McBride	0-3	0-2	0-0	2-1	1	0	1	0
Carter	0-0	0-0	0-0	0-1	0	0	0	0
Smith	1-4	0-0	0-0	1-1	0	0	0	2
Ingram	2-4	0-0	1-1	1-0	0	1	4	5
Totals	20-56 (35.7%)	7-22 (31.8%)	17-24 (70.8%)	19-26	11	4	11	64

Illinois guard Deron Williams said. "It was just a tragic thing for him and his family, and we're right there with him."

On Friday night, they were with him only in spirit. Weber spent the hours immediately after his mother's death at Rush University Medical Center, where she was taken from the United Center on Friday morning after feeling chest pains and where she died about 6 p.m. during surgery to repair a ruptured descending aorta.

Surrounded by family—brother David left to coach his own high school team, Glenbrook North, to a win—Weber mourned and began planning a funeral, plans for which he and his family intended to finalize sometime Saturday. It was at the hospital that Weber decided he would coach Saturday's game, a decision his team learned at a 9 p.m. meeting at its hotel.

"Basketball's been a major part of our life," Weber said. "She loved it. My dad loved it. (The

RIGHT: Dee Brown dribbles upcourt against Minnesota pressure. Brown and the Illini struggled to win an "ugly" game, 64-56. *Robert K. O'Daniell/The News-Gazette*

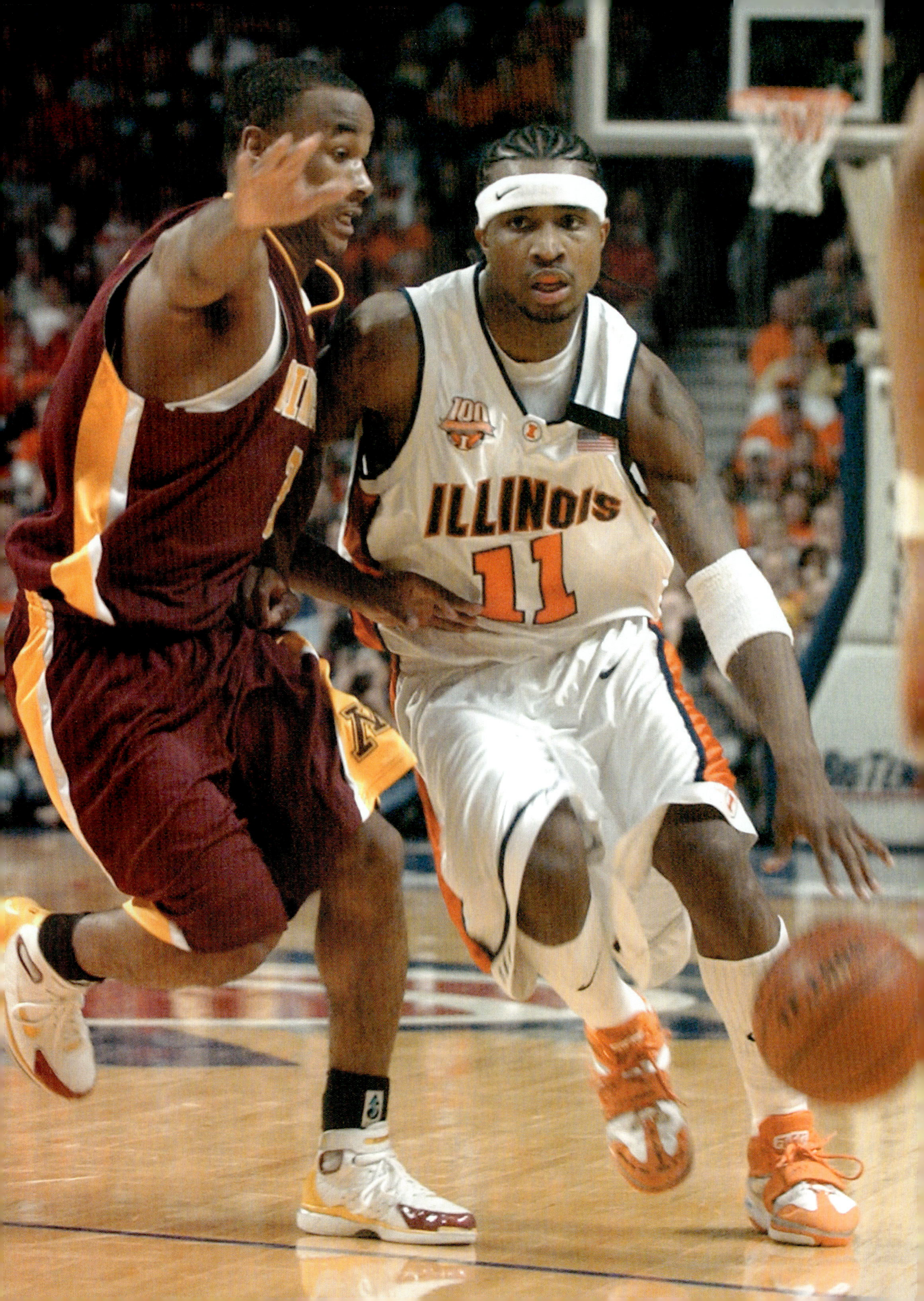
ILLINOIS
11

family) thought it would be the best thing to do."

In fact, Weber said, he was honoring Dawn Weber's wishes by coaching. As she was taken to the operating room, the last thing Dawn told her daughter was not to tell Bruce and David about her surgery.

"She thought we wouldn't coach as well as we could have," Bruce Weber said.

She'd had little cause for such concern this season. An avid Illinois convert, Dawn Weber had a satellite dish so she could watch her son coach every game from her home in Wisconsin. She took the Ohio State loss hard, Weber said, but soaked up all the good in one of the greatest seasons in Illinois basketball history.

"She just couldn't believe what had really happened with our team," Weber said. "She said to her it was a fairy tale. It's just amazing the amount of publicity we've gotten, the attention we've gotten. For her to see her son there, she was very, very proud, as she was of my other brothers and sister, also."

Weber's players met Dawn Weber only in passing, but they honored her Saturday, wearing black bands on their jerseys in her memory. Weber, his coaching staff and other Illinois athletic department employees wore orange-and-black ribbons put together by assistant athletic director Kathy Hug.

But Weber told his players to honor his mother's memory another way. In an impassioned speech before the game, the Illinois coach told his team to take a lesson from the heartache of the weekend.

"He was basically telling us you can't control life and death," Williams said. "But you can control what you go out and do every day and how hard you play on the court, so you should go out and play like it's your last game every game."

RIGHT: Dee Brown applies the defensive pressure to Minnesota's Aaron Robinson. The Illini forced 18 turnovers and collected 11 steals in the victory. *AP/WWP*

BELOW: Bruce Weber sports a ribbon on his jacket in honor of his late mother. It was an emotional day for Weber, but the game itself provided him an opportunity for a two-hour distraction from his grief. *Jonathan Daniel/Getty Images*

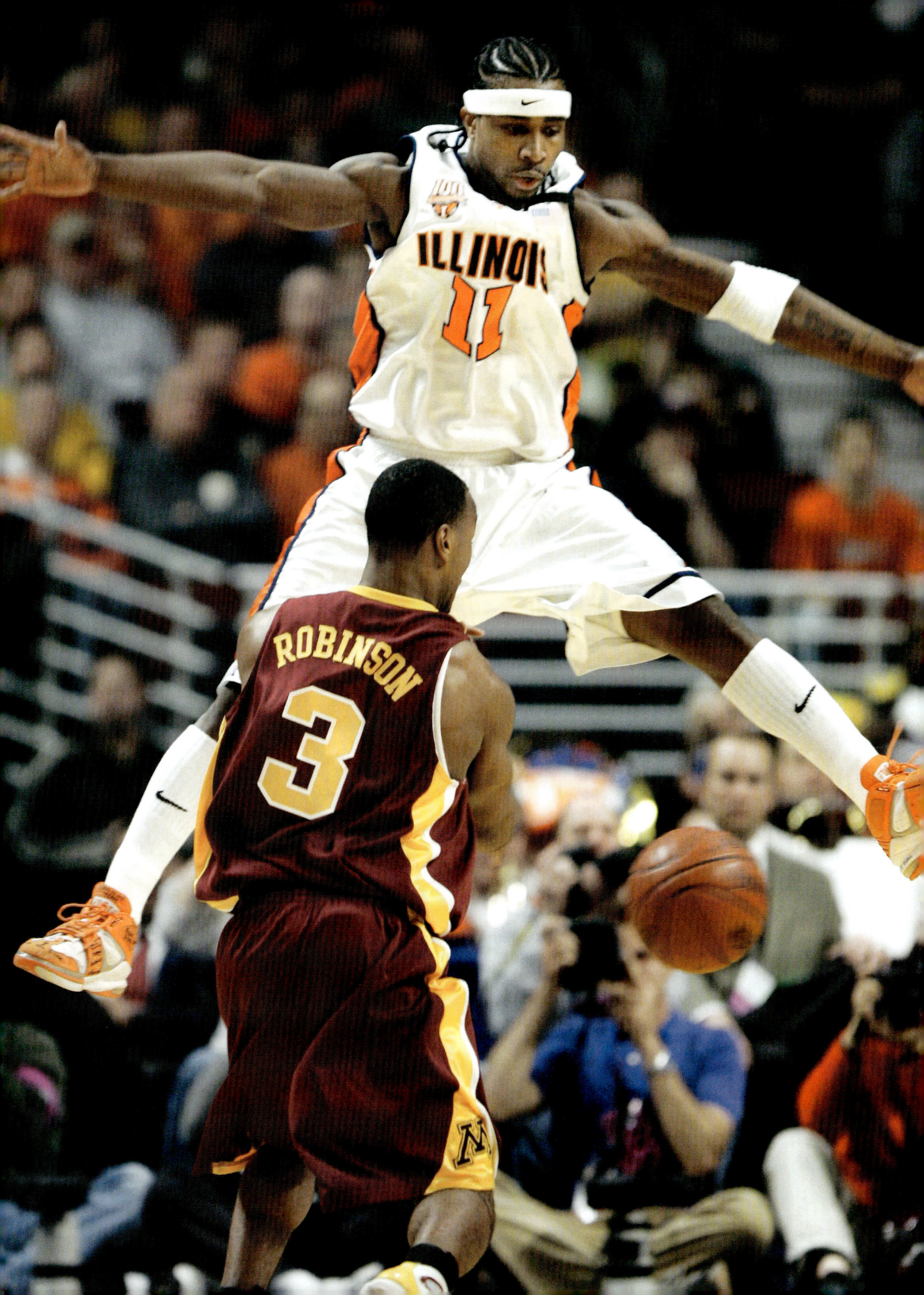
ILLINOIS
11
ROBINSON
3

BIG TEN TOURNAMENT, CHAMPIONSHIP   MARCH 13, 2005

United Center, Chicago, Illinois

ILLINI WIN TOURNEY THANKS TO MVP

BY BRETT DAWSON, *News-Gazette Staff Writer*

James Augustine was talking about food when they introduced him as the Big Ten tournament MVP on Sunday. Fitting, on a weekend when he ate the Big Ten alive.

"I was talking to Nick (Smith) about what was going to be for dinner in the meeting room," Augustine said after a 12-point, nine-rebound performance in a 54-43 Illinois win against Wisconsin in the tourney title game. "I had no idea (I would win the award). I was surprised with it."

Maybe the biggest surprise of the day, though, was that Augustine and Roger Powell Jr. dominated Sunday's game even as guards Dee Brown (0-for-8 shooting), Deron Williams (3 for 10) and Luther Head (2 for 8 from three-point range) continued to struggle. The end result—Augustine and Powell combined for 27 points and 21 rebounds—provided a measure of validation for an inside tandem that has spent most of the season as an afterthought.

Teams have been trying for weeks to apply extra pressure to the Illini in the backcourt, giving Augustine and Powell more room to operate on the inside. This weekend, they took advantage. In three games at the United Center, Augustine averaged 12.6 points and 10.3 rebounds a game. Powell averaged 12 and nine boards a game. That from a duo that entered the tournament without having scored in double figures in the same game since a February 16 rout at Penn State.

"At the beginning of the season, everybody questioned our big men," Williams said. "They've showed all year that they're definitely not our weakness. They're one of the strengths. It was good to see James get his confidence back and Roger get his confidence back because we're definitely going to need them in the (NCAA) tournament."

RIGHT: James Augustine, who was perfect from the floor in scoring 12 points, maneuvers around Wisconsin's Mike Wilkinson during the Illini's 54-43 victory in the championship game. *Robert K. O'Daniell/The News-Gazette*

Illinois 54 | Wisconsin 43

That tournament begins at 8:40 p.m. Thursday, when Illinois, the No. 1 seed in the Chicago Regional, will play 16th-seeded Fairleigh Dickinson at the RCA Dome in Indianapolis. UI coach Bruce Weber would like nothing more than to see his big men repeat their Big Ten tourney feats and watch his guards get back on track after a sloppy-shooting weekend.

But as long as the Illini (32-1) defend the way they did against Wisconsin on Sunday, Weber will like his chances. The Badgers scored 12 points in a 2-minute, 20-second stretch late in the second half to whittle a 16-point Illinois lead to five. But outside of that spurt, the Illini took the muscle out of Bo Ryan's flex offense. The Badgers shot 25.9 percent from the floor, and star Mike Wilkinson's eight points came on 1-for-7 shooting.

No surprise that afterward the credit for that defensive effort went primarily to Augustine and Powell, who blanketed Wilkinson and forced Wisconsin forward Alando Tucker to throw up wild shots. He finished 4 for 14 from the floor. Powell finished with 12 rebounds to go with his 15 points. Augustine blocked three shots.

"(Augustine) played extremely well and was very aggressive," Ryan said. "He made a statement in the paint. He intimidated our guys a little bit."

Augustine and Powell, meanwhile, didn't back down from anything all weekend. Powell, Weber said, came into the weekend with "a little bit of a chip on his shoulder" after he was left off all three All-Big Ten teams. Augustine, a third-team all-conference selection, had something to prove after averaging 6.7 points during the last three games of the regular season. And all season, the Illini's flashy backcourt trio has overshadowed Illinois' inside duo.

"I always thought we'd hold up our end of the bargain," Powell said. "We've been competing hard, playing defense, guarding bigger players. That's something we've done well, I believe, all year."

	1st	2nd	Total
Wisconsin (#19)	18	25	43
Illinois (#1)	26	28	54

Wisconsin

Player	FGM-A	3FGM-A	FTM-A	O-D REB	A	BLK	S	TP
Hanson	2-3	2-3	0-0	0-1	0	0	1	6
Tucker	4-14	1-3	0-0	1-2	0	1	0	9
Wilkinson	1-7	0-1	6-6	1-7	4	1	0	8
Chambliss	2-7	1-5	0-0	0-1	2	0	1	5
Taylor	2-9	2-3	2-2	0-3	2	0	0	8
Nixon	1-3	0-0	0-0	1-0	0	0	0	2
Morley	2-8	1-2	0-0	1-6	2	0	0	5
Helmigk	0-0	0-0	0-0	0-0	0	0	0	0
Flowers	0-2	0-1	0-0	0-5	1	0	0	0
Butch	0-1	0-1	0-0	0-1	0	0	0	0
Totals	14-54	7-19	8-8	9-27	11	2	2	43
	(25.9%)	(36.8%)	(100.0%)					

Illinois

Player	FGM-A	3FGM-A	FTM-A	O-D REB	A	BLK	S	TP
Head	5-12	2-8	0-0	1-4	4	0	1	12
Powell Jr.	3-10	2-3	7-8	5-7	0	0	0	15
Augustine	5-5	0-0	2-2	0-9	1	3	0	12
Williams	3-10	2-4	0-2	0-4	3	0	0	8
Brown	0-8	0-5	0-0	0-3	5	1	1	0
McBride	1-1	1-1	0-0	1-0	0	0	0	3
Carter	0-0	0-0	0-0	0-0	0	0	0	0
Smith	0-1	0-0	0-0	0-0	0	0	0	0
Ingram	2-6	0-1	0-0	0-1	0	1	1	4
Totals	19-53	7-22	9-12	9-31	13	6	3	54
	(35.8%)	(31.8%)	(75.0%)					

They carried the Illini this weekend, leading Illinois to its second Big Ten tournament title in three seasons and giving Weber his first title—a happy ending to a heartbreaking weekend for the coach, whose mother, Dawn, died Friday in Chicago.

Weber seemed more relaxed Sunday, joking with CBS announcers after the game and taking the microphone during a postgame celebration to tell the thousands of Illinois fans who stayed in the stands, "We have a good problem. We're running out of places to put trophies in our office." The Illini hope to have to clear out some space for another big one in three weeks at the conclusion of the NCAA tournament.

RIGHT: Roger Powell Jr., who scored 15 points and snagged 12 rebounds, shoots over Alando Tucker.
Robert K. O'Daniell/The News-Gazette

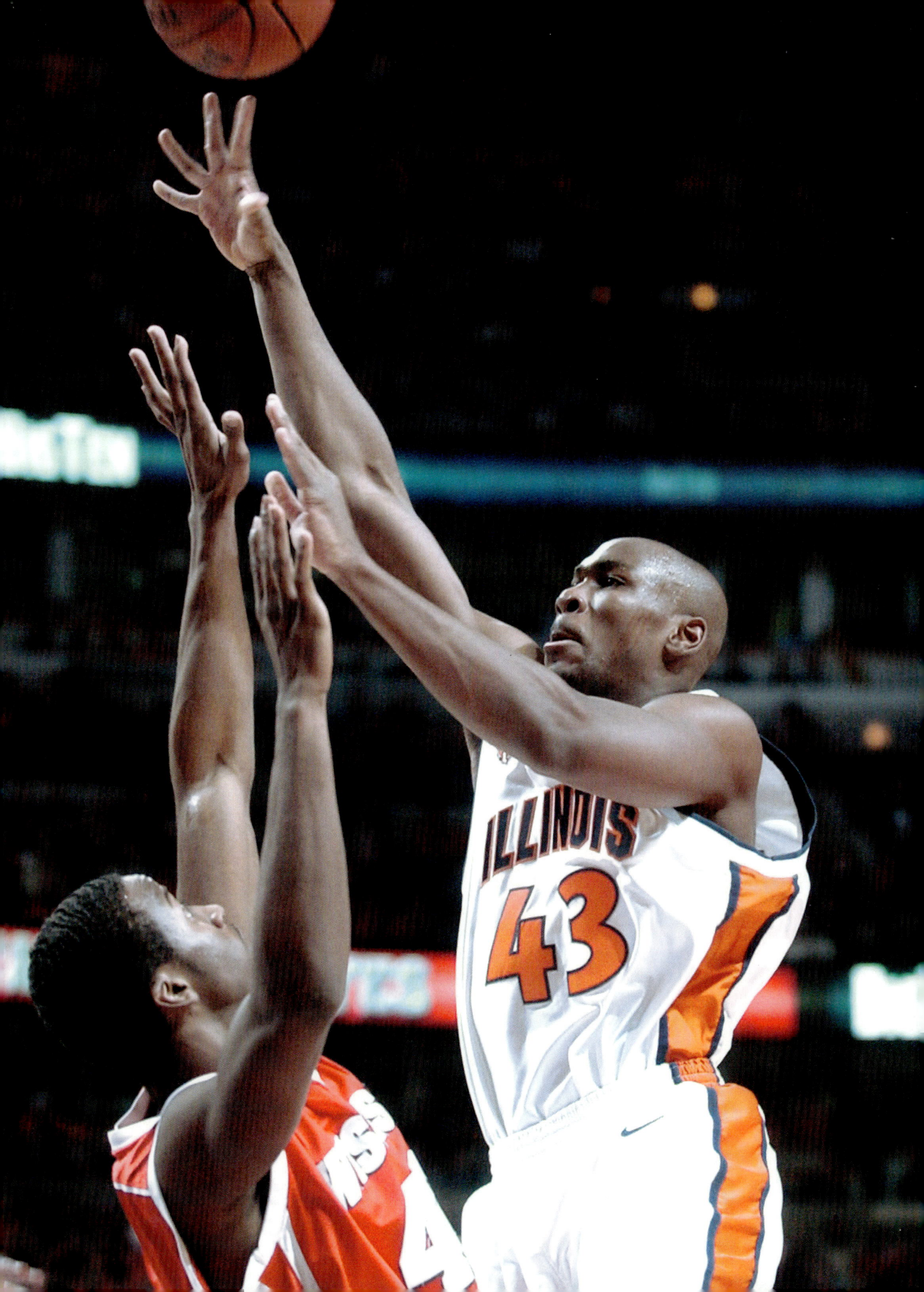
ILLINOIS
43

NCAA TOURNAMENT, ROUND 1   MARCH 17, 2005

RCA Dome, Indianapolis, Indiana

KNIGHTS TAKE THE FIGHT TO ILLINI

BY BRETT DAWSON, *News-Gazette Staff Writer*

The boisterous point guard had just made a deep three-pointer to beat the halftime buzzer, and he tucked his thumbs under his jersey, lifting so everyone in the RCA Dome could see his school's name.

The point guard was Tamien Trent, not Dee Brown. But Trent's Fairleigh Dickinson team, for a half at least, did a pretty fair Illinois impression here in the first round of the NCAA tournament Thursday, dominating inside, pounding the backboards and trailing by a single point in what eventually turned into a 67-55 win.

Illinois survived and advanced to Saturday's 4:40 p.m. tipoff against No. 9 seed Nevada. But Thursday's halftime score—Illinois 32, Fairleigh Dickinson 31—must've turned a few heads across the nation. In the Illini locker room, some were hanging.

"Angry," guard Deron Williams said when asked to describe Illinois' halftime emotions. "We felt we should be playing better. Embarrassed. That's a team we felt like we should've beaten handily."

Almost everyone—including the orange-clad majority in the crowd of 28,604—thought they would do just that. Instead, the halftime chatter was about if Illinois possibly could end up on the wrong side of history. No team seeded No. 1 has lost to a 16 seed in the NCAA tournament.

Bruce Weber's halftime message was hardly cheery.

"We just said we were disappointed," Weber said. "We had so many mental breakdowns with little things we normally don't do."

The Illini don't normally get dominated in the paint (the Knights had a 20-10 scoring advantage there at halftime) nor get completely battered on the boards (despite James Augustine's career-high 15 rebounds, Illinois was outrebounded 42-30). And No. 1 seeds—particularly those favored to win the NCAA tournament—don't normally flirt with disaster on Day 1.

RIGHT: Tamien Trent and his Fairleigh Dickinson teammates gave Luther Head and the Illini more of a game than they expected. *John Dixon/The News-Gazette*

Illinois 67 | Fairleigh Dickinson 55

"We've had a tendency against teams that don't have maybe quite the reputation (to not) play great basketball all the time," Weber said. "We have a tendency to let up."

That tendency reared its ugly head in the first half, when Illinois led 30-20. At that point, Williams went to the bench with two fouls and Illinois quickly found itself in a game. The Knights (20-13) ripped off an 11-2 run that stunned the Illini and sent the college basketball-viewing public into a tizzy. At sports bars and tourney sites across the nation, folks must have wondered if it could really happen. In the RCA Dome, the Illini didn't allow the thought to cross their minds.

"It wasn't going to happen, not in the first round," center Nick Smith said. "It might happen against Nevada, but not in the first round. I didn't even think about the possibility."

The possibilty didn't exist very deep into the second half. Fueled by Brown, who scored 10 of his 18 points in a quick burst after halftime—including four on what he called "two of the luckiest shots ever," a runner that was tipped in by a Fairleigh Dickinson player and an awkward baseline bank—Illinois charged out to a 13-point lead six minutes into the half. The Illini (33-1) cruised from there, leading by as many as 19 with 5:14 to play.

There's a breeze that swirls in the RCA Dome sometimes. Late Thursday night, it felt a little like a giant sigh of relief—at least from Illinois fans. Weber swears, though, that he wasn't tense, that he didn't once think, "I can't be the first coach ever to do this."

"I think (I felt) more disappointment than relief, in that we wanted to play better," Weber said. "But you're always leery. If you don't win, it's going to end, and I think this was a little bit of a wake-up."

And Weber figures his team needed it. Nevada has shown its tournament moxy already, advancing to the Sweet 16 last year and upsetting Texas 61-57 on Thursday even without a big game from star Nick Fazekas.

Asked if his team can run with Illinois, Wolf Pack coach Mark Fox chuckled.

	1st	2nd	Total
Fairleigh Dickinson	31	24	55
Illinois (#1)	32	35	67

Fairleigh Dickinson

Player	FGM-A	3FGM-A	FTM-A	O-D REB	A	BLK	S	TP
Klaiber	11-20	2-5	0-1	4-4	0	0	2	24
Crosariol	2-3	0-0	2-2	4-4	1	3	0	6
Timberlake	2-7	0-1	0-2	1-1	1	0	1	4
Peterson	1-7	0-3	0-0	1-6	2	0	0	2
Trent	4-9	1-5	2-4	1-4	5	0	1	11
Harris	2-5	0-0	0-0	0-1	0	0	0	4
Peeples	0-5	0-1	0-0	1-3	1	0	1	0
Murray	0-0	0-0	0-0	1-3	1	0	1	0
Cousins	0-0	0-0	1-2	0-0	0	0	0	1
Buch	1-1	1-1	0-0	0-0	0	0	0	3
Totals	23-57	4-16	5-11	15-27	11	3	6	55
	(40.4%)	(25.0%)	(45.5%)					

Illinois

Player	FGM-A	3FGM-A	FTM-A	O-D REB	A	BLK	S	TP
Augustine	2-5	0-0	7-11	3-12	0	1	0	11
Powell Jr.	2-4	1-1	0-0	1-2	1	0	2	5
Head	4-15	3-8	2-2	1-0	5	0	1	13
Williams	3-9	0-4	2-2	0-2	6	0	2	8
Brown	7-10	2-5	3-4	0-1	2	0	1	19
McBride	0-2	0-2	0-0	0-1	0	0	1	0
Carter	1-1	0-0	1-2	0-0	0	0	0	3
Smith	1-3	0-0	0-0	0-1	1	0	0	2
Ingram	3-5	0-1	0-0	1-2	1	1	1	6
Pruitt	0-0	0-0	0-0	0-0	0	0	0	0
Totals	23-54	6-21	15-21	8-22	16	2	8	67
	(42.6%)	(28.6%)	(71.4%)					

"No," he said. "We can't walk with Illinois, either. I'm not sure what we can do with Illinois, other than look at the flag with them for the national anthem. They're great."

They didn't look that way Thursday. But whatever caused Illinois' flirtation with history—first-game nerves, dome jitters, the burden of expectations—the Illini vowed it was a one-time problem. A fixable one.

"Thank God we got it out of the way now," Roger Powell Jr. said. "We've got to pick it up next game and play Illinois basketball, the way we're capable of playing."

RIGHT: Dee Brown sparked the Illini on to victory with a team-high 19 points. *John Dixon/The News-Gazette*

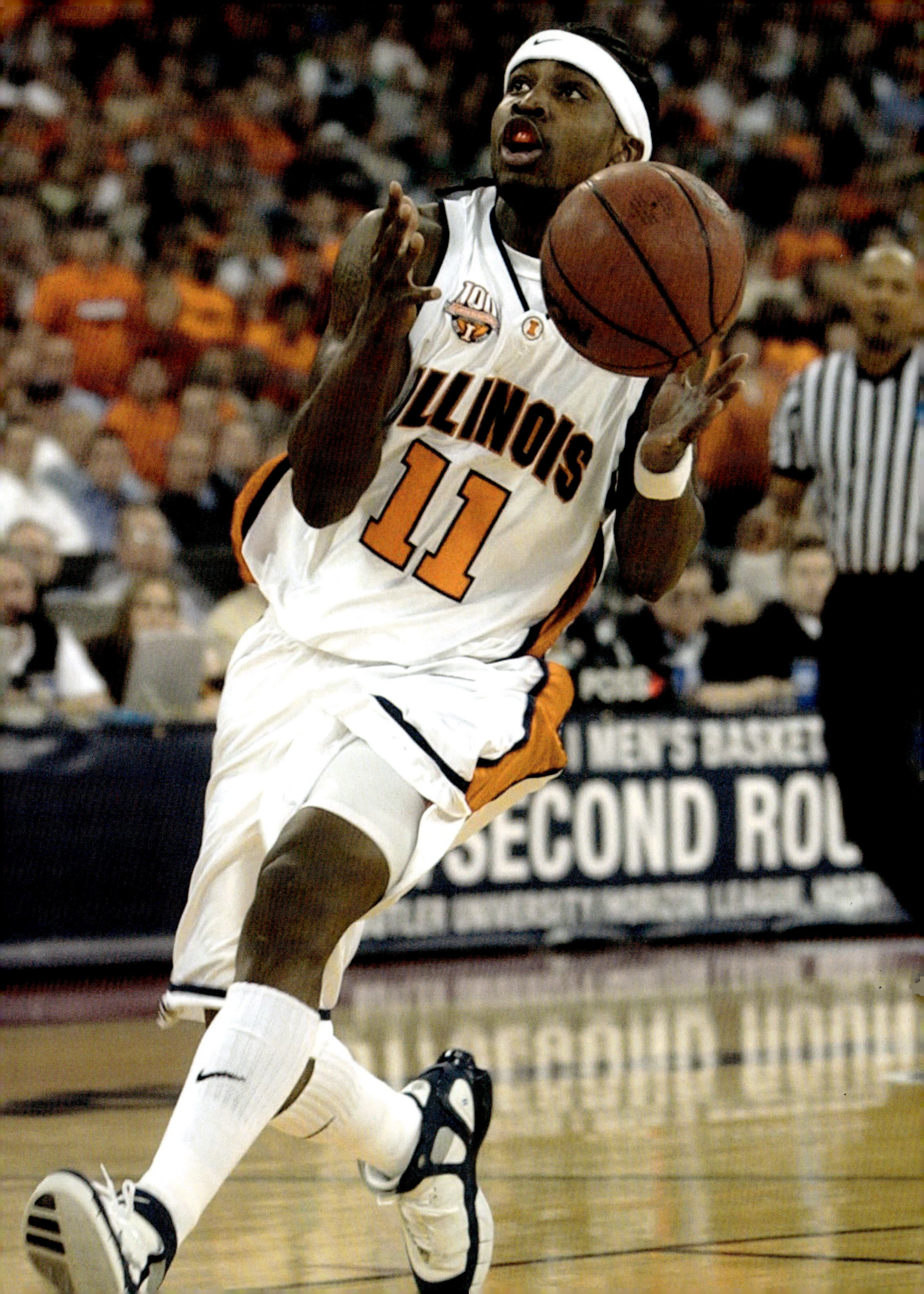
ILLINOIS
11

NCAA TOURNAMENT, ROUND 2 MARCH 19, 2005

RCA Dome, Indianapolis, Indiana

THE REAL ILLINI STAND UP

BY BRETT DAWSON, *News-Gazette Staff Writer*

Illinois spent much of the regular season being compared—sometimes unfavorably—to North Carolina. The Illini bristled when a national media type said the Tar Heels were the superior team, even as the wins piled up in Champaign-Urbana. Bruce Weber's players didn't much like the comparison. So imagine their surprise Saturday, when their coach made it himself.

"Did anybody see Carolina play at the beginning of the game (Friday night)?" Weber asked his team. "Guys are diving into the stands, they're making plays, screaming, yelling. We haven't had that. We need to do that."

On Saturday, the top-seeded Illini did just that, storming into the NCAA tournament's Sweet 16 with a 71-59 win against No. 9 seed Nevada at the RCA Dome. For one night at least, it looked like the Illini of old were back.

"Today we were happy and having fun and playing together," Illinois guard Luther Head said.

The result was Illinois' most dominating performance since late in the regular season, a game the Illini controlled from the opening moments of the second half. As a result, Illinois (34-1) is off to meet Wisconsin-Milwaukee—Weber's alma mater and home to former Iowa thorn-in-the-side Bruce Pearl—on Thursday in the Sweet 16 at Allstate Arena in Rosemont.

Nevada (25-7) was determined to keep Illinois' guards bottled up, but that meant leaving plenty of room for the Illini big men to roam. And on a night when Illinois looked like its old fun-loving self, nobody had a better time than James Augustine (a career-high 23 points, 10 rebounds) and Jack Ingram (12 points, also a career high).

"They gave those guys a lot of space to work with," guard Dee Brown said. "We just got 'em the ball, got 'em involved. Everybody got in on the act tonight."

For the first time in six games, it was a high-wire act. Illinois shattered its offensive slump, shooting 53.1 percent (its first game better than 50 percent since a regular season win March 3 against Purdue. The Illini also cracked the 70-point mark for the first time since that game. The numbers alone didn't tell the story.

RIGHT: James Augustine scores on an unchallenged dunk early in the game. Augustine put together a career game with 23 points, 10 rebounds, four steals and two blocks. *Darrell Hoemann/The News-Gazette*

Illinois 71 | Nevada 59

To appreciate Illinois' reversal of offensive fortune, you had to see the spring in its collective step, the dormant swagger that woke up during a nine-minute stretch in which the Illini outscored the Wolf Pack 21-7 and held Nevada without a field goal. Illinois dashed and slashed during that stretch, and though it still was without its familiar old three-point shooting eye (the Illini hit a season-low two in 12 attempts), Weber's team looked like the team that dominated the regular season. And with every basket and stop, every rebound and steal, the orange-wearing majority in the crowd of 40,331 roared its approval.

"Once we got the run, the crowd started to get into it, we got some transition—everything started clicking," Weber said.

Still, it wasn't the kind of near-flawless basketball the Illini played in January and February. There was that off-the-mark three-point shooting. And there was a seven-minute stretch late, when Nevada went to a zone defense, in which Illinois didn't put the ball in the basket, its only points coming on a goaltended jumper by Deron Williams. That dry spell let Nevada trim a 22-point lead to nine with 1:41 to play, but Illinois pulled away with free throws down the stretch and walked off the court feeling like the Final Four favorite it had been until recent games.

"We were just disappointed in our play against Fairleigh Dickinson," Williams said. "We wanted to come out and show everybody who the real Illinois is."

The junior guard did his part, finishing with 15 points and 10 assists and serving as the straw that stirred Illinois' offensive orange drink. But it was Augustine—motivated, his teammates said, by a *News-Gazette* graphic on Saturday that gave Nevada's Nick Fazekas the edge in a head-to-head matchup—who stole the Illini show, finishing with his second consecutive NCAA tournament double-double.

After the game, the Illini kept the celebrating to a minimum, staying true to what they'd proclaimed Friday: The Sweet 16 is a path, not a destination, a steppingstone to a higher goal.

	1st	2nd	Total
Nevada	27	32	59
Illinois (#1)	34	37	71

Nevada

Player	FGM-A	3FGM-A	FTM-A	O-D REB	A	BLK	S	TP
Pinkney	7-12	2-3	6-6	3-8	0	0	2	22
Fazekas	5-20	0-4	1-2	1-6	0	0	2	11
Washington	0-2	0-0	2-5	3-0	0	0	0	2
Shiloh	3-5	1-1	0-0	1-0	1	0	2	7
Sessions	1-3	0-0	2-2	1-1	7	0	0	4
Charlo	4-9	0-1	4-8	2-1	2	1	3	12
Taylor	0-0	0-0	0-0	0-1	0	0	0	0
Bell	0-3	0-0	1-1	1-2	0	0	1	1
Totals	20-54	3-9	16-25	12-20	10	1	10	59
	(37.0%)	(33.3%)	(64.0%)					

Illinois

Player	FGM-A	3FGM-A	FTM-A	O-D REB	A	BLK	S	TP
Augustine	9-11	0-0	5-5	1-9	0	2	4	23
Powell Jr.	2-7	0-1	1-2	0-3	0	0	2	5
Head	5-9	2-6	2-3	0-4	3	0	0	14
Williams	4-9	0-1	7-8	0-4	10	0	0	15
Brown	0-4	0-3	2-2	1-3	5	0	0	2
McBride	0-0	0-0	0-0	0-0	0	0	0	0
Carter	0-0	0-0	0-0	0-1	0	0	0	0
Smith	0-2	0-0	0-0	1-0	0	0	0	0
Ingram	6-7	0-1	0-0	2-1	0	1	3	12
Totals	26-49	2-12	17-20	5-26	18	3	9	71
	(53.1%)	(16.7%)	(85.0%)					

But they wore familiar faces in the locker room afterward, the smiles and loose body language reminiscent of the team that walloped Wake Forest and manhandled Michigan State on the road.

Forget the Carolina comparisons. Illinois is just happy to look like Illinois again.

RIGHT: Jack Ingram scored a career-high 12 points in the game and added three steals, three boards and a block. *Darrell Hoemann/The News-Gazette*

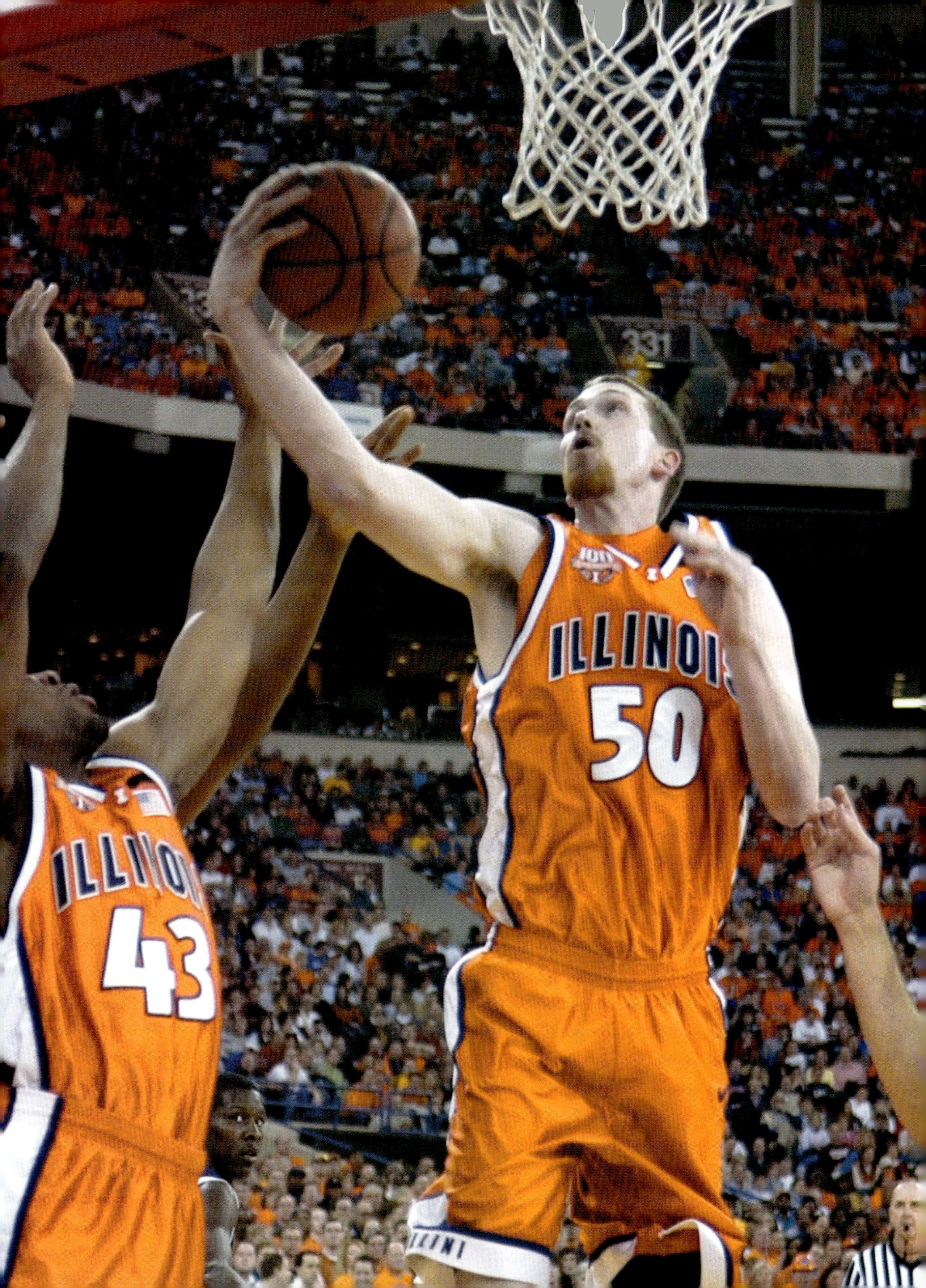
ILLINOIS
50
ILLINOIS
43
331

NCAA TOURNAMENT, SWEET SIXTEEN   MARCH 24, 2005

Allstate Arena, Rosemont, Illinois

ON TO THE FIELD OF EIGHT

BY BRETT DAWSON, *News-Gazette Staff Writer*

Maybe you can't wait. There's one game now between Illinois and the Final Four, and maybe you can't stand the wait. Maybe Thursday's 77-63 Illinois win against Wisconsin-Milwaukee in the Sweet 16 has you counting the hours until Saturday.

Dee Brown has counted them, too. He doesn't like the math.

"I wish we had two, three more days," Brown said in the Illinois locker room Thursday night. "I'm tired, man."

Too bad for Brown that he'll suit up sooner. The Illini get Arizona at 6 p.m. Saturday, less than 48 hours after dispatching the Panthers and Bruce Pearl in a game more hotly contested than a 14-point spread says.

The seeds say this has been an easy road for Illinois. If the Illini should win Saturday and go on to win the national championship, its path to the Final Four would be among the easiest of any champ ever. The Illini aren't so sure. Yes, top-seeded Illinois has played a 16 seed and a 9 and on Thursday handled a No. 12. But don't suggest the Illini, who have won their three NCAA tournament games by an average of 12.7 points, have had it easy.

"Obviously, the teams we're playing are beating the other teams, so they're good," Brown said. "It ain't no fluke. Wisconsin-Milwaukee beat (Alabama and Boston College) handily. It's not a cakewalk for us. We've probably got the hardest road now of any team."

It looked that way Thursday, Arizona outlasting Oklahoma State in one of the hardest-fought and most entertaining games of the tournament. The Illini (35-1) know the knock, that it's been months since they played anyone as good as the Wildcats, that they aren't tested in a tight game against a tough opponent, that their tournament road thus far was straight and easily navigated.

"That'll be our test, (to see) if we're ready to play," forward James Augustine said.

If Illinois advances to St. Louis and wins the championship, it will match the easiest-seeded road to the Final Four of any champion since seeding began in 1979. Only Arkansas in 1994 won the title after reaching the Final Four with wins against teams seeded 16th, ninth, 12th and third. But, don't tell Bruce Weber that. Don't suggest it's been an easy road so far.

RIGHT: Dee Brown raises the defensive intensity during the first half of the Illini's 77-63 victory over the Panthers. Brown scored 21 points, connected for five three-pointers and added two steals in the game.
Darrell Hoemann/The News-Gazette

Illinois 77 | **Wisconsin-Milwaukee 63**

"There were other teams—good teams—that that had easy teams in the first round, and they lost," Weber said. "The difference is we just took care of business."

That's become a theme for the Illini. Wisconsin-Milwaukee (26-6), with its fullcourt press and a red-hot Joah Tucker, put up a fight Thursday night, running with the Illini early and keeping them from pulling away late. Tucker had 32 points, and the Panthers hung tough.

But Brown was vintage Brown, from the three-point line (where he was 5 of 8) to the postgame news conference, where he slipped Weber a cup of water and whispered to his coach, "I stuck my finger in it." And Deron Williams matched him play for play, taking over the game in stretches, dishing out a game-high eight assists and matching Brown with 21 points. Afterward, though, there was little celebration—smiles and laughs all around, sure, but few fist-pumps or chest bumps.

"They've been very businesslike," Weber said. "And they're very drained. It was a hard-fought game. Deron said he looked at the clock at seven minutes and thought it just stopped and never moved again."

If the Panthers took that much out of the Illini, how much is left? What does Illinois have in reserve for Arizona (30-6), with sharpshooting guard Salim Stoudamire coming off a 19-point performance in which he dropped the game-winning basket on Oklahoma State?

"We'll be ready," Williams said.

After all, there's plenty at stake. Illinois has been to the Elite Eight one time since its 1989 Final Four run, and that trip ended with a loss to Arizona. That means Illinois has been in this position once in 16 years. None of the current players—nor the current coach—have played with this much on the line.

But if the Illini aren't prepared for what's ahead, if they're concerned about taking a step up in level of competition, they aren't showing it.

"It feels good to know we've got one game here out of the way," said guard Luther Head,

	1st	2nd	Total
Wisc.-Milwaukee	32	31	63
Illinois (#1)	39	38	77

Wisconsin-Milwaukee

Player	FGM-A	3FGM-A	FTM-A	O-D REB	A	BLK	S	TP
Tucker	12-18	2-3	6-8	1-2	1	0	1	32
Tigert	1-6	0-3	0-0	1-6	2	1	1	2
Hill	0-3	0-3	2-3	0-4	4	0	0	2
McCants	4-17	4-14	1-2	2-2	3	0	2	13
Davis	3-9	1-5	2-2	3-2	0	2	0	9
Pancratz	0-0	0-0	0-0	1-2	0	0	0	0
McCoy	1-3	0-1	1-2	2-0	2	0	0	3
Wright	1-1	0-0	0-1	3-2	0	0	0	2
Totals	22-57	7-29	12-18	13-22	12	3	4	63
	(38.6%)	(24.1%)	(66.7%)					

Illinois

Player	FGM-A	3FGM-A	FTM-A	O-D REB	A	BLK	S	TP
Augustine	3-3	0-0	5-6	1-9	0	1	0	11
Powell Jr.	5-11	0-1	2-2	5-4	1	0	1	12
Head	5-15	2-5	0-1	0-1	6	0	2	12
Williams	8-12	2-5	3-4	0-3	8	0	1	21
Brown	7-12	5-8	2-2	0-2	2	1	2	21
McBride	0-1	0-1	0-0	0-0	0	0	0	0
Carter	0-1	0-0	0-0	0-1	2	0	0	0
Smith	0-0	0-0	0-0	0-0	1	0	0	0
Ingram	0-2	0-0	0-0	1-1	0	0	1	0
Totals	28-57	9-20	12-15	8-25	20	2	7	77
	(49.1%)	(45.0%)	(80.0%)					

who scored 12 points and hit a crucial late three-pointer despite playing on a sore hamstring. "But it's not over yet."

The Illini are hoping it's not even close.

"We're playing good basketball," Weber said. "We'll see on Saturday if it's our best."

RIGHT: A good sign for Illini fans: Deron Williams, who scored 21 points and dished out eight assists, smiles during a break in action in the second half.
Jonathan Daniel/Getty Images

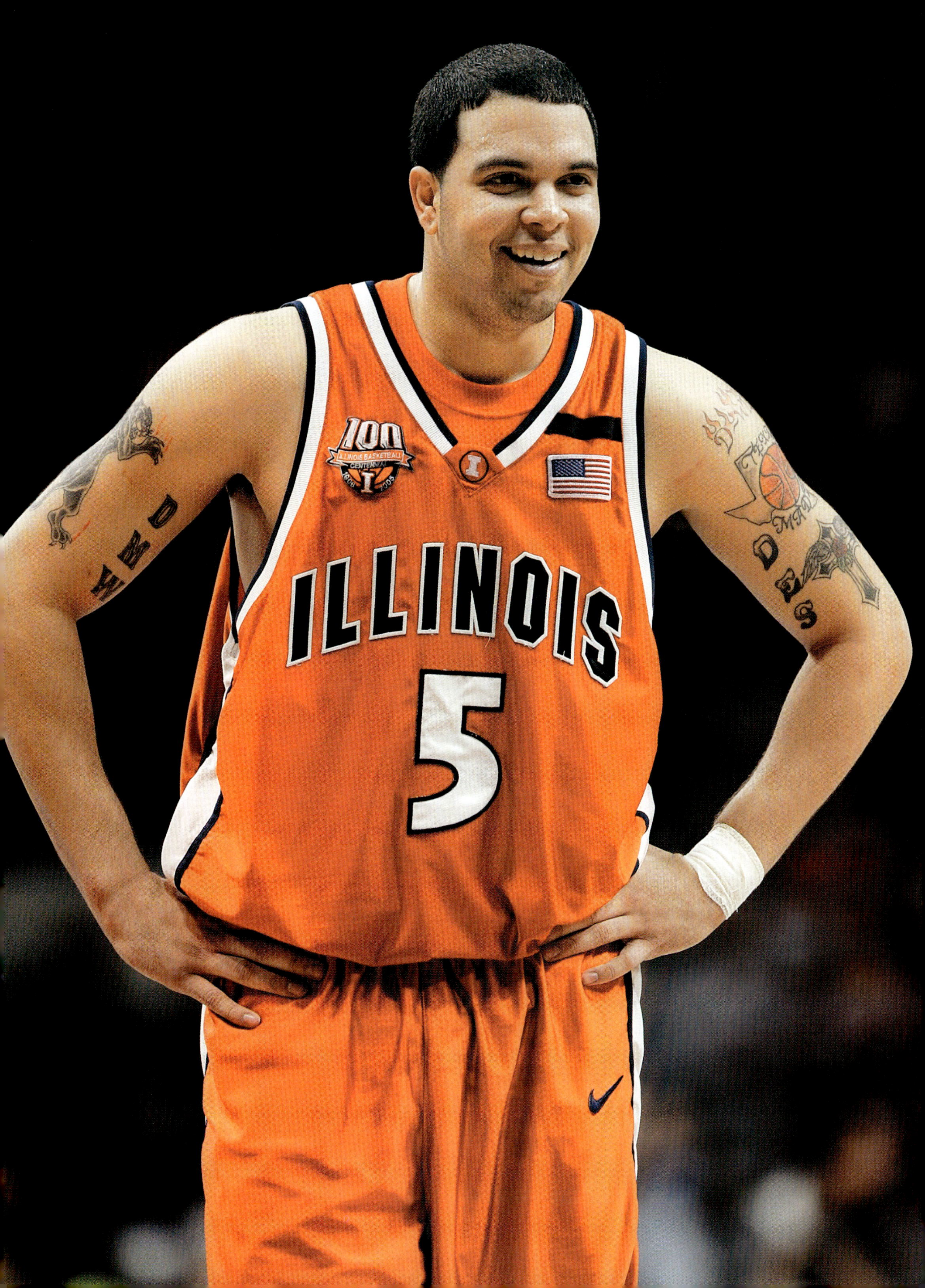
ILLINOIS
5

NCAA TOURNAMENT, ELITE EIGHT   MARCH 26, 2005
Allstate Arena, Rosemont, Illinois

THE WILL TO WIN

BY BRETT DAWSON, *News-Gazette Staff Writer*

He broke down amid the bedlam, tears streaming down his cheeks and sweat creeping through his suit. Bruce Weber, the loudest man in the business, was at a loss for words. And why not? How could he comprehend the scene he'd seen? What words were there for what happened Saturday night in the Chicago Regional final, for Illinois' 90-89 overtime win against Arizona? How could Weber be expected to grasp what his team did in charging into Illinois' first Final Four since 1989?

For the Illini—down 15 with four minutes, four seconds to play in regulation, trailing 80-72 with 63 seconds left on this magical season—to rally and win? Language failed Weber. There were only tears—and hugs.

"I thought of my mom. I did," Weber said. "I thought of my mom and dad, and all the sacrifices they made so I could get here. It's been so emotional these last couple of weeks, it was just … you can't describe it."

Across the court from Weber—and celebrating in stark contrast to his restrained reaction—was his demonstrative duo of point guards. At the top of his lungs, though the sound still was swallowed in the din of Allstate Arena, Dee Brown shouted to Deron Williams, "I told you! I told you!"

"I told him he was the best guard in the country, and he was going to dominate down the stretch," Brown said minutes later. "And that's exactly what he did."

But if Brown knew that it could go this way, that Williams would score eight of his 22 points in the final 3:52, that the burly junior would net six more in overtime, then his precognitive powers are even more dazzling than his fantastic fast breaks.

Illinois beat Arizona on Saturday night, and if you missed it, you'll never forgive yourself. But don't worry. You'll see it replayed for years. "A classic game," Illinois athletic director Ron Guenther called it, and who could argue?

Thirty-six minutes of game time had passed, and Illinois was toast. Nine minutes later, the Illini were the toast of Champaign. Illinois outscored Arizona 20-5 in the last four minutes of regulation, the capper coming on a Jack Ingram steal and a Williams three-pointer with 38.2 seconds remaining that tied the game at 80 and gave Illinois a chance to make a defensive stand.

RIGHT: The shot: Arizona's Channing Frye rushes to cover Deron Williams as he releases the game-tying three-pointer that sent the contest to overtime, where the Illini won, 90-89. *Doug Benc/Getty Images*

Illinois 90 | Arizona 89

All season, the stars seemed in the proper Illini alignment, with the school's basketball centennial falling in a season its roster was stocked with talent. The road to St. Louis included stops in Indianapolis and Chicago, short drives from Champaign, and Illinois seemed a team of destiny. Never has that theory had legs like it had Saturday night.

"I looked at the other guys' eyes (during timeouts), and they were like, 'It ain't over. We've still got to fight,'" Brown said. "The way everyone was acting in the huddle, it was like we were still fired up and we still could do it. I never panicked because I felt like we had a chance."

It hardly looked that way. For most of the second half, Arizona dominated. Even as Williams put the clamps on Arizona's leading scorer Salim Stoudamire, the supporting Wildcats stepped into a starring role. Channing

BELOW: The Illinois bench goes wild after Deron Williams nailed the game-tying three-pointer that would send the game to overtime. *John Dixon/The News-Gazette*

ABOVE: Deron Williams picked a great time to have his career-defining game. He made an array of clutch shots in scoring 22 points to lead Illinois' come-from-behind victory against Arizona. *John Dixon/The News-Gazette*

ABOVE: Roger Powell Jr. and Jack Ingram celebrate as the horn sounds in the Illini's come-from-behind, overtime victory against Arizona. *John Dixon/The News-Gazette*

Frye controlled the paint en route to a 24-point night. Hassan Adams, guarded most of the night by a limping Luther Head—still feeling the effects of a strained hamstring—scored inside and out and finished with 21.

And with time running short and Arizona's lead expanding, Adams turned to Stoudamire, slapped his hand and said, "Five minutes to St. Louis." At the same time, Weber was telling his team not to believe it.

"I said, 'You guys have worked way too hard to quit. You have to keep fighting,'" Weber said. "And they did. The whole game, all the bounces went (Arizona's) way, then all of the sudden, the bounces started going our way."

Then Weber's message started to sink in. He told his players, "Look at my eyes," and urged them to focus. Somewhere, Illinois found something in reserve. It came from Head's hustle and Brown's defense. It came from Williams' determination, and from the riotous sound of the crowd of 16,957, all but a pocket decked out in orange.

"I was just screaming at my teammates not to give up," Head said.

Weber did the same. On the inside, though, he wasn't as confident. In the long hallway outside Illinois' locker room, the coach admitted there was a time, trailing by 15 with time ticking away, that he thought about the end of this wild ride, considered the possibility that a team he's come to love would have no tomorrow.

"At one point, I was like, 'What am I going to say to everybody (if we lose)?'" Weber said. "I told them afterward, 'I didn't have a good speech for you, so I'm glad I get to tell you we're going to the Final Four.'"

Illinois heads there this week after 16 years of failed attempts. A date awaits with Rick Pitino and Louisville, a team about which Weber admitted he knows "almost nothing."

Scouting starts today.

"I told our coaches, 'Go have a dang beer,'" Weber said.

There's reason to celebrate. Weber's first thought in the aftermath was of his mother, Dawn, who died three weeks ago during heart surgery. His first hug was from Gary Nottingham, the assistant to the head coach who spent years as a Division II coach. It took time before he could utter his first words. But after he'd shed his last tear, Weber wore a smile that displayed pride and joy and more than a little relief, and once he'd gathered his head, he couldn't stop talking about his Final Four-bound team's heart.

"They have toughness and competitive spirit," Weber said. "I told them, 'We got a miracle, guys. Now we have an opportunity.' I think the pressure is in getting (to the Final Four).

"Now we're there; let's go win the national championship."

	1st	2nd	OT	Total
Arizona (#9)	36	44	9	89
Illinois (#1)	38	42	10	90

Arizona

Player	FGM-A	3FGM-A	FTM-A	O-D REB	A	BLK	S	TP
Adams	9-13	1-3	2-3	4-4	5	0	1	21
Radenovic	4-6	1-1	4-4	1-4	2	1	4	13
Frye	11-14	1-1	1-2	3-9	1	6	0	24
Shakur	4-6	2-3	2-2	1-1	4	0	2	12
Stoudamire	2-13	1-7	4-4	0-5	7	0	2	9
McClellan	2-7	1-2	5-6	2-2	1	1	1	10
Rodgers	0-2	0-1	0-0	0-0	1	0	1	0
Walters	0-0	0-0	0-0	0-0	0	0	0	0
Totals	32-61	7-18	18-21	12-25	21	8	11	89
	(52.5%)	(38.9%)	(85.7%)					

Illinois

Player	FGM-A	3FGM-A	FTM-A	O-D REB	A	BLK	S	TP
Augustine	1-3	0-0	2-4	3-3	1	0	2	4
Powell Jr.	6-11	1-3	3-3	4-1	0	1	0	16
Head	7-18	5-12	1-2	0-3	2	1	4	20
Williams	8-15	5-9	1-2	0-3	10	0	1	22
Brown	6-14	3-8	0-0	2-3	7	0	3	15
McBride	1-2	1-2	0-0	0-1	0	0	0	3
Carter	0-0	0-0	2-2	1-1	0	0	0	2
Ingram	3-8	1-1	1-2	2-1	1	0	2	8
Totals	32-71	16-35	10-15	14-18	21	2	12	90
	(45.1%)	(45.7%)	(66.7%)					

CHECK FOR A PULSE BEFORE BURIAL

BY LOREN TATE, *News-Gazette Columnist*

March 26, 2005

"I still don't know what happened," puzzled a weary but still healthy Luther Head.

"It's all a blur," a drenched Bruce Weber said.

Excuse these numbed participants because this Team of Destiny just got tapped by Lady Luck's wand in the most remarkable basketball game, considering the stakes, in 100 years of Illini history.

What happened was a miracle finish—"Praise the Lord," bellowed Rev. Roger Powell Jr., "He does make miracles."—in a shocking 90-89 overtime triumph that kept the title drive alive.

Even the roaring orange clads in the Allstate Arena crowd of 16,957 began to lose hope when Arizona stormed ahead 75-60, and the Wildcats had the basketball and a 77-68 lead with 1:30 to go.

New York's Dick Weiss and other big-city scribes were poised to bury Illinois with their computers. They were already writing their leads. Illinois had lost. Illinois wasn't that good in the first place. Illinois hadn't defeated anybody worth note. Illinois couldn't handle a team with a quality big man. Illinois depends too heavily on three-pointers.

Then lightning struck. Head's steal made it 77-70 with 1:21 showing. In the huddle, the gritty UI players tried to convince each other they still had a chance.

"I said if it's going to be, it will happen," Dee Brown said.

"Coach said, 'If we're going down, let's go down fighting,'" Deron Williams said.

That's how they tied it, and then they almost broke it open in overtime when the UI's 12th steal shook Head for a breakaway and 90-84 spread. But what will become known as the greatest game in Illini history, even surpassing the twin victories against Louisville and Syracuse in 1989, didn't end there. Junior Hassan Adams hauled Arizona within one and had the ball at the top of the circle with 10 seconds left.

Okay, take your hands from your eyes. You can look. Adams couldn't create anything against the rugged Williams and wound up missing badly a rushed shot at the end.

Hard to Believe

So what if they permitted a season-high 89 points? So what if they couldn't head off Adams and couldn't handle the magnificent Frye? This was a game salvaged by heart and desperation. And when it counted, by poise.

"Arizona was in control for so much of the time," Weber said. "We didn't have any answers for them. We couldn't stop them. What happened was just amazing."

That's what makes it so special. On this day, Illinois defeated a clearly superior opponent. On this day, Arizona ruled both ends and had the game in hand, and Illinois simply came charging out of nowhere to steal it away. When the game had structure, Arizona ruled. When the game became a blurry hodge-podge, the score swung in Illinois' favor.

Under the circumstances, with the March to the Arch in such dire jeopardy, no Illini team has ever experienced anything quite like it. A charmed team continues to live a charmed life at 36-1. Bring on your best wordsmiths. Haul out your juiciest adjectives. Don't hold anything back. This was the epitome.

And what a crowd. What incredible support. What delirious joy. Only a determined security force, so intent that officers tried to prevent new fan Bill Murray from walking across for a halftime radio interview, prevented a massive postgame pileup at midcourt. The fans couldn't join the melee, but they stood and cheered for another 20 minutes while the Illini high-fived and cut down the nets.

It doesn't get any better than this. Not that the Illini are satisfied but, please Bruce, give them a day or two to let this one sink in. Like Powell said, Somebody Up There had a hand in this one.

Enjoy Easter. These are the days.

BELOW: Luther Head (right) embraces teammate Dee Brown during the postgame celebration. *Doug Benc/Getty Images*

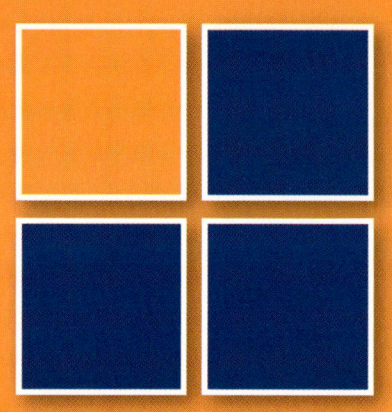

CARLE CLINIC ASSOCIATION PROUDLY CONGRATULATES THE FIGHTING ILLINI MEN'S BASKETBALL TEAM

Fighting Illini Basketball is a legacy storied with successful teams, amazing players and great coaches. But most of all, it's a legacy of fond memories. Thank you for making the 2004 - 2005 season the most memorable of all.

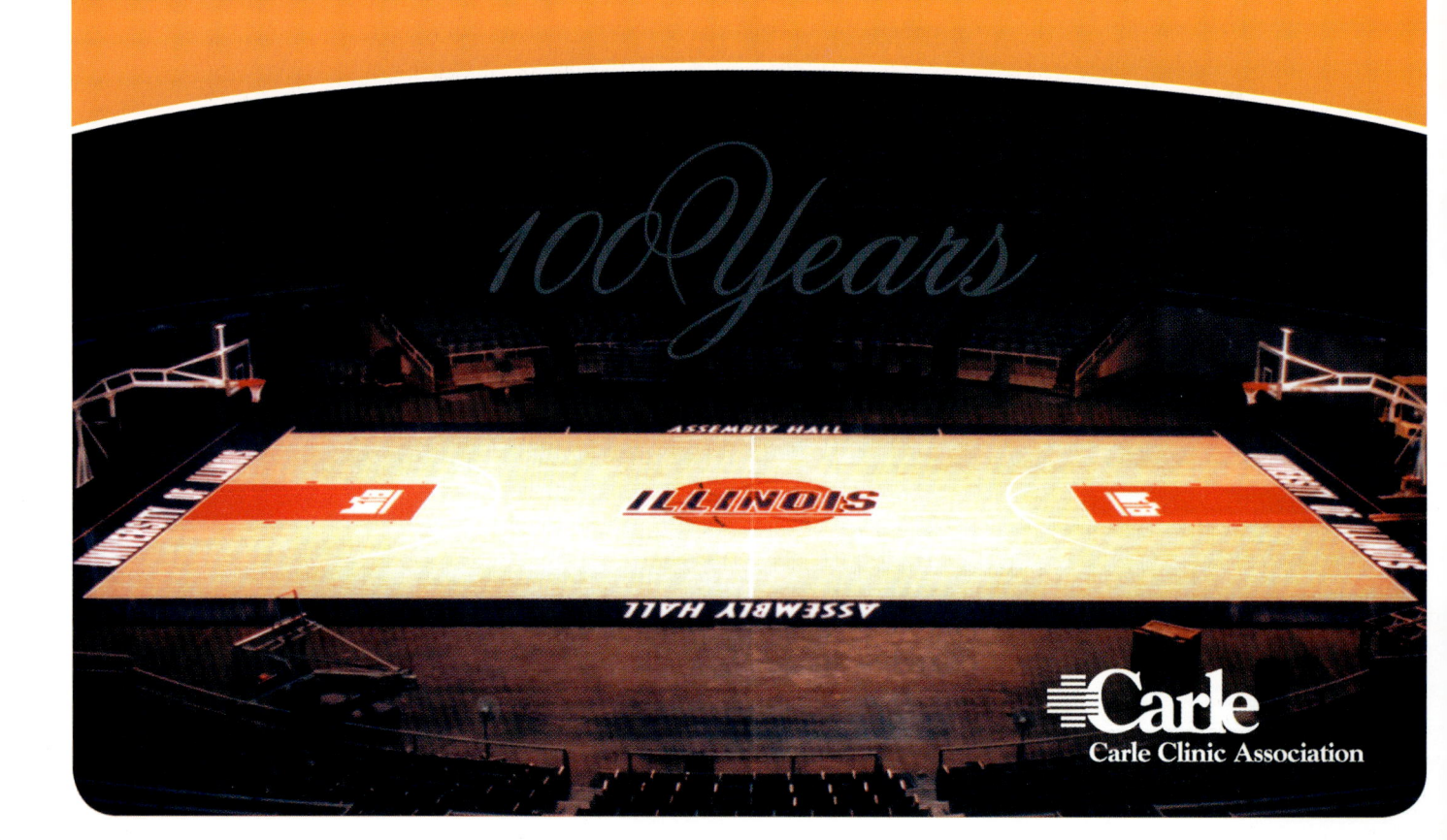

100 Years

Carle
Carle Clinic Association

Train. Practice. Compete. Win. Repeat as necessary.

For some, sports provide a personal sense of achievement. For others, it's the thrill of competition. And for others, it's all about being part of the team. But no matter why you play sports, you don't just learn how to be a better athlete. You learn to be a better person. And as a network of agents dedicated to teamwork and taking care of people, we're proud to sponsor athletes of all ages — no matter what drives them to succeed. WE BELIEVE IN THE POWER OF SPORT.

Kenneth E Davenport Agency
Urbana, IL 61801
kdavenpo@amfam.com
(217) 344-5171

Charles W Bridges III Agency
Urbana, IL 61801
cbridge4@amfam.com
(217) 344-4785

Toni M Tolch Agency
Urbana, IL 61802
ttolch@amfam.com
(217) 337-4988

Bradley L Shipp Agency
Champaign, IL 61821
bship1@amfam.com
(217) 351-8285

Jim Bishop Agency
Champaign, IL 61821
jbishop@amfam.com
(217) 359-6645

Perry D Ford Agency
Champaign, IL 61820
pfor2@amfam.com
(217) 356-5952

Marilyn L Blanzy Agency
Champaign, IL 61822
mblanzy@amfam.com
(217) 355-6221

Brian M Morin Agency
Champaign, IL 61822
bmorin@amfam.com
(217) 355-9929

Jeffrey L Stipp, Agent
Danville, IL 61832
jstip1@amfam.com
(217) 442-8120

Cynthia K Barrett Agency
Bourbonnais, IL 60914
cbarrett@amfam.com
(815) 932-0923

Craig A Page Agency
Bradley, IL 60915
cpag2@amfam.com
(815) 929-0924

Scott Kibler Agency Inc
Tuscola, IL 61953
skibler@amfam.com
(217) 253-2731

Dwight Unzicker Agency
Mahomet, IL 61853
dunzicke@amfam.com
(217) 586-4090

Philip D Norfleet Agency
Monticello, IL 61856
pnorflee@amfam.com
(217) 762-2136

Mark Anderson Agency
Monticello, IL 61856
manders4@amfam.com
(217) 762-4721

Thanks for 100 Years of Exciting Fighting Illini Basketball!

AMERICAN FAMILY INSURANCE
All your protection under one roof

© 2005 American Family Mutual Insurance Company and its Subsidiaries
Home Office - Madison, WI 53783 • www.amfam.com • AD-000916 Rev. 2/04

NCAA TOURNAMENT, FINAL FOUR APRIL 2, 2005

Edward Jones Dome, St. Louis, Missouri

ILLINI TAKE THEIR GAME TO A HIGHER PLACE

BY BRETT DAWSON, *News-Gazette Staff Writer*

Three hours away, fans were losing their minds in the streets of Champaign. But in the depths of the Edward Jones Dome, in the expanse of the top seed's locker room, the Illinois basketball team was subdued. There were high-fives and hugs—nothing that required riot gear.

The Illini beat Louisville 72-57 on Saturday in an NCAA semifinal game to set up their first trip to the national championship game. But you'd hardly know it based on the reaction.

"We wanted to act like we've been there before," Illinois guard Deron Williams said. "Even though we haven't."

Illinois is in uncharted territory now, its 8:21 p.m. Monday date set with North Carolina in a title game that since midseason has seemed almost predestined. Getting there required a methodical, precise win against Rick Pitino's Cardinals, a game Illinois (37-1) won by outscoring Louisville 41-29 on 62.5 percent shooting in the second half.

The postgame scene was as businesslike as the win that set it off. Roger Powell Jr. celebrated perhaps the finest moment of his career—a 20-point game and an 18-point second half—by pointing to the sky in a show of faith, then marching off the court with his teammates.

"We didn't come in here and do any flips or nothing," said guard Luther Head, who matched Powell's game-high 20 points. "We came in here and gave each other high-fives, but we know on Monday we still have work to do."

Work the Illini can handle. It's play the Illini haven't done too much of lately. Though it's a stretch to say this has been a season deprived of joy, the last few weeks have been short on pleasure. Between the death of Bruce Weber's mother and the ever-present pressure to cap a historic season with a Final Four run, Illinois rarely has

---

RIGHT: Roger Powell Jr. gestures after the Illini defeated the Cardinals, 72-57. He had a game for the ages, scoring 18 points in the second half to spark Illinois on to victory. *John Dixon/The News-Gazette*

Illinois 72 | Louisville 57

looked unburdened. But a funny thing happened on the way here.

"I think there was more pressure on us just to get to the Final Four," said Williams, who scored five points, dished out nine assists and helped stifle Cardinals star Francisco Garcia. "Once we got here, it was a little more relaxed. We didn't come out tense at all."

Instead, the Illini put the pressure on Louisville with a 12-0 second-half run that broke open a close game and sent the Cardinals (33-5) home from their first Final Four appearance in 19 years. Illinois carved up the Cards' defense, forcing Pitino to pull out of his 2-3 zone into a man-to-man that the Illini exploited inside.

Powell was a revved-up Reverend in the second half, the licensed minister playing like a man possessed after halftime. He tossed in two three-pointers and rebounded his own miss of another for a monster dunk. That paced a frontcourt attack that accounted for 39 points, including nine off the bench from Jack Ingram.

"That's been the story of the Illinois season," Williams said. "Somebody steps up. Every game, it's a different guy."

Maybe there is an "I" in team. A big, orange one.

"They truly are a great team," Pitino said. "I don't know if they necessarily had the greatest talent I've seen from a Final Four (team), but they're the best team I've seen in some time."

On Monday night—for the first time—that team plays for a national championship.

"We're there. We're one of two," Weber said. "They're very deserving of being there. They've earned it with what they've done all year—not just the tournament, but all year. They should feel good about themselves."

But not too good.

"We don't want to be satisfied," forward James Augustine said.

Satisfaction would come Monday, with a win against North Carolina (32-4), an 87-71 winner against Michigan State in Saturday's second national semifinal. Roy Williams' team spent most of the season on the Illini's tail in the

	1st	2nd	Total
Louisville (#4)	28	29	57
Illinois (#1)	31	41	72

Louisville

Player	FGM-A	3FGM-A	FTM-A	O-D REB	A	BLK	S	TP
Myles	8-12	0-0	1-1	3-4	2	3	2	17
Palacios	0-0	0-0	0-0	1-3	1	0	0	0
Garcia	2-10	0-4	0-0	0-1	2	1	1	4
Dean	4-15	2-9	2-2	0-1	1	0	1	12
O'Bannon	4-10	2-5	2-2	0-4	4	0	0	12
Jenkins	2-3	2-2	2-2	0-2	0	0	1	8
George	1-4	0-0	2-5	3-3	0	0	0	4
Wade	0-0	0-0	0-0	0-0	0	0	0	0
Totals	21-54	6-20	9-12	7-18	10	4	5	57
	(38.9%)	(30.0%)	(75.0%)					

Illinois

Player	FGM-A	3FGM-A	FTM-A	O-D REB	A	BLK	S	TP
Augustine	1-3	0-0	4-6	2-9	0	0	0	6
Powell Jr.	9-13	2-3	0-0	4-1	2	0	1	20
Head	6-13	6-11	2-2	0-6	5	0	2	20
Williams	2-7	1-5	0-0	0-5	9	0	0	5
Brown	3-10	2-9	0-0	0-3	4	0	1	8
Ingram	4-6	1-1	0-0	3-2	1	0	0	9
McBride	0-1	0-1	0-0	0-1	0	0	0	0
Carter	0-0	0-0	0-0	0-0	0	0	0	0
Smith	2-3	0-0	0-0	0-0	0	0	0	4
Totals	27-56	12-30	6-8	9-27	21	0	4	72
	(48.2%)	(40.0%)	(75.0%)					

national polls, inspiring countless debates on the subject of the nation's best. On Monday, the two will settle it on the court.

Illinois' fans were in the streets on Saturday night. The Illini were ready to hit the sheets.

"We're going to rest up and get ready to play again," Williams said.

One more game, and if the Illini win that one, they'll celebrate like their fans. Until then?

"All the stuff we've accomplished this year, getting (to the title game) just feels like just another thing on the resume," Augustine said.

"Hopefully we've got one more step on Monday."

ABOVE: Luther Head was part of the stellar senior effort for the Illini against Louisville. Head chipped in 20 points, nailed six three-pointers, and added six rebounds, five assists and two steals. *John Dixon/The News-Gazette*

SENIORS LEAD THE WAY

BY LOREN TATE, *News-Gazette Columnist*

April 2, 2005

How do you figure? In a Halloween-like clash of Illini orange and Louisville black Saturday, three extraordinary Illinois juniors combined for one meaningless field goal in the last 25 minutes of the most important game of their lives.

That's Dee Brown, the "face" of NCAA basketball; Deron Williams, a sure-fire first-rounder in the NBA draft; and James Augustine, the MVP of the Big Ten tournament.

One basket. Plus three free throws. Five points in a Final Four showdown. And yet there was little doubt as to the outcome. The giant orange-clad fandom in the packed Edward Jones Dome barely broke a sweat. Louisville hung close for 30 minutes and cashed in with barely a whimper, 72-57. The Cardinals managed eight points in the last 10 minutes.

It is one more example of this team's remarkable, sometimes inexplicable sense of sharing, a quality of bubbling chemistry that has carried Bruce Weber's forces into Monday's national championship game against North Carolina.

It is exactly where they belong. They have set the table with a scattershot of heroic performances. Look here and they hit you there. It was Roger Powell Jr.'s turn Saturday. And Luther Head's. They grabbed the Cardinals by the throat shortly after intermission and left them dangling. Those two gritty seniors split 40 points down the middle.

Powell sat out 15 minutes in the first half before going on a rampage with 12 of Illinois' first 14 points after the break. It reminded of his sterling finish a year ago when he bagged 22 against Cincinnati and 15 in a season-ending loss to Duke. Head, meanwhile, drained six three-pointers to match the total of a Louisville team that had lived by the trey. In the final count, four UI seniors of this supposedly junior-led team produced 53 points, almost enough to whip the Cardinals by themselves.

"Our juniors are great," Weber said, "but I said all along that we'd only go as far as our seniors could take us. They stood up tonight and got us to the championship game."

Breaking Through

So Monday, with the miraculous rally against Arizona still ringing in their ears, the Illini will attempt to finish off their spectacular thrill ride. It already is the deepest advancement in UI basketball history, Harry Combes' three Final Four teams losing in the semifinal round, and Lou Henson's Flyin' Illini falling to Michigan in Seattle. The last three Final Four losses came by an agonizing two points in games that could have turned either way in the closing seconds.

Illinoisans have had to live with those disappointments. Weber's athletes didn't leave any doubt Saturday. After shooting too many three-pointers (19) and drawing too few fouls (five) against Louisville's 2-3 zone in the first half, they conspired to force the ball inside thereafter.

After a prayerful intermission, a fresh Powell was ready to take up the challenge. He erupted, even blasting in to dunk his own missed three-pointer. When Head converted Williams' feeds for back-to-back treys, Illinois was on an 11-0 run that had Louisville gasping, 61-49, under the six-minute mark. The Illini, after shooting 37.5 percent in the first half, cashed 15 of 24 fielders for 62.5 marksmanship thereafter.

No excuses Monday. They have no limping Efrem Winters or ailing Kenny Battle as they reach this chance-of-a-lifetime showdown in the same near-perfect health that they've enjoyed throughout a 37-1 season. They couldn't be in a better mental frame, the entire squad confident that Dee and Deron are poised to break out as they often do after a chilly (5 of 17) performance. And they can count on a strong bench effort from Jack Ingram, who has grown to the point where he is as valuable as a starter.

Words Can't Describe It

Like Lute Olson before him, Louisville coach Rick Pitino poured out accolades.

"So many times, you say, 'What if?' when it's over," Pitino said. "You look back on a few key plays that could have changed the outcome. But in this case we had to pitch a perfect game.

"We hung in as long as we could, and then we lost. We had to zone primarily because we had a limited bench inside, and we knew it would be difficult to stop them from penetrating. If we played them 10 times, they'd win eight or nine."

Pitino said Francisco Garcia will be an outstanding pro, but "he got caught taking difficult shots early, and it mushroomed on him. We were close at halftime (31-28), and yet he felt like he wasn't contributing enough."

Garcia, a junior, went 2 for 10, sounding like another athlete who feared his NBA first-round status was slipping and let it get to him. Williams was too much for him, shutting him down while dishing out nine assists on the other end.

"One thing I found," Weber said, "is if we assign Deron to a really top player, he takes pride in his defense. He tends to relax when we put him on a lesser scorer. He's smart, and he has a big body, and he got help from our bigs on the screens."

Now comes the matchup the nation has been waiting for. Let the drum roll begin.

RIGHT: Coach Bruce Weber had his team ready for Rick Pitino's Cardinals. The Illini advanced to the championship game for the first time in school— and Weber's—history.
John Dixon/The News-Gazette

NCAA TOURNAMENT CHAMPIONSHIP   APRIL 4, 2005

Edward Jones Dome, St. Louis, Missouri

ILLINI DON'T GO DOWN WITHOUT FIGHT

BY LOREN TATE, *News-Gazette Columnist*

The magical ride ended Monday night. Bruce Weber's 37-2 Illini traveled further than any Illinois team in history, fought all the way back from their second 15-point deficit in the NCAA tournament, but ultimately bowed to North Carolina's firepower, 75-70, in a riveting championship game.

So they lost, but not before they tied the game at 65-all and 70-all, not before they outfought the Tar Heels with 17 offensive rebounds, and not until they missed their last six three-pointers with the orange-clad fans going wild in the monster crowd of 47,262.

There is nothing to be sad about, not when these Illini rallied so relentlessly, not when they performed with such courage. In 66 years, no team ever came back from a 13-point halftime deficit in the championship game, but Illinois got all the way back to tie it before finishing with the same cold hand they began with.

Coach Roy Williams' first championship team was strikingly efficient with 27 baskets in 52 shots. By contrast, the Illini missed 43 fielders, the most since their overtime win against Iowa on Jan. 20, and settled for subpar 38.6 percent accuracy. We'll chew on two major issues for many months: (1) the ability of Sean May, a college-sized Shaq, to dislodge UI defenders by throwing his 260 pounds into them for easy baskets; and (2) the emphasis on three-pointers by an Illini team that launched 40 of 70 shots from beyond the arc.

Do Onto Others ...

It's always nervous time when you see the biggest game in UI history is officiated by three mystery men. No Steve Welmer. No recognizable ref. Let's emphasize first that most of May's baskets were legitimate. He is incredibly agile for a big bear. But with Illinois ahead 17-16, May backed straight over Roger Powell Jr. for a no-

RIGHT: Sean May was too much in the middle for the Illini to handle. He scored 26 points, despite the enormous efforts of Roger Powell Jr. and Jack Ingram to contain him. *Ronald Martinez/Getty Images*

North Carolina 75 | Illinois 70

call layup. He saw what was permitted and took advantage of his beef.

Later on, when a furious Illini rally cut the lead to 52-50, May brought it back to 57-50 by barging straight through and over the outsized Powell for a three-point play and a basket. Nor was James Augustine around to help. He fouled out in nine minutes of playing time, shaking his head repeatedly at the nickel-and-dime nature of his misdeeds.

The only answer to this blatant defiance of the game's rules is to get a beefy guy like May and do the same thing in return. It'll be Weber's job to take young Georgian Charles Jackson or one of the returning UI huskies (Shaun Pruitt or Marcus Arnold) and teach them to do the same thing. Better someone complains about Illinois defying the rules by being too physical than vice versa.

Just like Shaquille O'Neal in the NBA, May did what these officials, and most of their compatriots, allow. So, if it is okay to charge in the post, the only solution is to do the same in return. Referees simply don't protect slender centers who lack the physical strength to prevent heavier rivals from backing them down. Illinois lost because May made 10 of 11 shots and scored 26 points, and the margin probably

	1st	2nd	Total
North Carolina (#2)	40	35	75
Illinois (#1)	27	43	70

North Carolina

Player	FGM-A	3FGM-A	FTM-A	O-D REB	A	BLK	S	TP
J. Williams	3-6	3-4	0-0	1-4	0	1	1	9
McCants	6-15	2-5	0-0	1-1	1	0	1	14
May	10-11	0-0	6-8	2-8	2	1	0	26
Felton	4-9	4-5	5-6	0-3	7	0	2	17
Manuel	0-1	0-0	0-2	0-3	2	0	0	0
M. Williams	4-8	0-1	0-1	3-2	0	0	0	8
Noel	0-0	0-0	1-2	1-2	0	0	0	1
Scott	0-2	0-1	0-0	0-2	0	0	0	0
Terry	0-0	0-0	0-0	0-0	0	0	0	0
Thomas	0-0	0-0	0-0	0-1	0	0	0	0
Totals	27-52 (51.9%)	9-16 (56.3%)	12-19 (63.2%)	8-26	12	2	4	75

Illinois

Player	FGM-A	3FGM-A	FTM-A	O-D REB	A	BLK	S	TP
Augustine	0-3	0-0	0-0	1-1	0	0	0	0
Powell Jr.	4-10	1-2	0-0	8-6	1	0	1	9
Head	8-21	5-16	0-0	1-4	3	1	2	21
Williams	7-16	3-10	0-2	0-4	7	0	1	17
Brown	4-10	2-8	2-2	0-4	7	0	3	12
Ingram	4-9	1-3	2-2	5-2	0	0	0	11
McBride	0-0	0-0	0-0	0-0	0	0	0	0
Carter	0-1	0-1	0-0	1-0	0	0	1	0
Smith	0-0	0-0	0-0	0-0	0	0	0	0
Totals	27-70 (38.6%)	12-40 (30.0%)	4-6 (66.7%)	17-22	18	1	8	70

LEFT: Bruce Weber lets the ref have it in the second half. Fouls doomed the Illini's interior defense, causing James Augustine to foul out and allowing Sean May to have his way in the paint. *John Dixon/The News-Gazette*

RIGHT: James Augustine was reduced to team cheerleader for most of the game. Augustine fouled out after playing just nine minutes. *John Dixon/The News-Gazette*

would have been wider if Carolina had gotten him the ball in the last four minutes.

Off the Mark

As was the case in last year's tournament loss to Duke, the Illini had reasonably open opportunities but couldn't connect. You'll be able to get a better explanation for this from our national media experts. They'll say—and Weber might agree—that Illinois shot too quickly, took too many three-pointers (40) and didn't go inside enough. That'll be the accepted opinion.

Not here. Who would the Illini go inside to? Augustine? He wasn't around long enough to make an impact and lacked the moves to score against those Carolina giants anyway. Jack Ingram and Powell? They are battlers (an incredible 13 offensive boards) but were obliged by Carolina's long arms to be step-out jump shooters for the most part.

Illinois supposedly had the best guard trio in the country and needed it to shoot well from the perimeter to win this game. It didn't. When the game broke open for the first time with Carolina forging ahead 23-17, Illinois was 4 of 12 on two-pointers and 3 of 12 on three-pointers. Before halftime, the inept shooting carried over into other areas. The Illini played 78 halves of basketball this season, and the 29 percent shooting was the worst.

Others will put some great meaning on these misses, perhaps inferring that Carolina's defense somehow caused three great UI guards to miss 24 of 34 three-pointers, and all six at the end. The real answer is they are human. Maybe we've tried to make them something else, but they're not. Deron Williams and Dee Brown have had more than one off night. So has Luther Head. It happens. The shame is that they carried the Illini banner so far, over the hills and through the valleys, and uplifted a fandom like no athletic team in Illini history. They had three open treys that could have given them the lead at the end. Sometimes the ball just won't go in.

In the final analysis, it was one of the great championship games and hopefully one that Weber and the Illini can use to their advantage.

115

TREASURE THE JOURNEY, IF NOT THE DESTINATION

BY BRETT DAWSON, *News-Gazette Staff Writer*

April 4, 2005

He will have forever for what-ifs, to think about the open shot that didn't go down or the first half that got away. But sitting there slumped in his locker at the Edward Jones Dome, Deron Williams said he won't.

He won't beat himself up over the open three-pointer on the wing. He won't lose sleep after coming this far and not finishing the job. By the time he met the media Monday night in the wake of Illinois' 75-70 loss to North Carolina in the NCAA championship game, Williams had shed any tears he planned to shed.

"Of course I'm sad—I'm sad that it's over, that we lost," Williams said. "But we did great things this year. We got to the Final Four. We played for the national championship. Maybe some people who weren't too excited about Illinois basketball are excited now."

You would expect the Illini to wear long faces in the locker room. You would expect them to cry, and they did. But before the Tar Heels had finished picking confetti out of their hair, Bruce Weber already broke his first smile of the night. It wouldn't be his last.

Weber hoped he—not Carolina's Roy Williams—would win his first national championship Monday night. He wanted desperately to finish what Illinois started with its historic run through one of college basketball's finest seasons. And he cried Monday night. He cried Sunday, too, during his team's last meeting of the year. He didn't want the journey to end, he said time and time again Monday.

"But how can you be sad?" Weber said. "If you're sad, you're sad that the journey's over, not about this game. We played a great team. We gave a great effort. We went down fighting. I'm not saying I didn't want to win the game. But if you're sad about this, I feel sorry for you. It doesn't get any better than this."

He meant this season—a 37-2 masterpiece that fell five points shy of completion—but Weber might have been talking about Monday's game, a national final that will live in memories for some time.

"It was a great game," Illinois guard Dee Brown said. "But you know, somebody had to lose it."

A season that so often was a downhill charge ended with an uphill climb for Illinois,

---

RIGHT: Luther Head and the vaunted perimeter game for the Illini came up just short in the championship game. The team shot just 30 percent from beyond the arc, despite launching 40 attempts. *John Dixon/The News-Gazette*

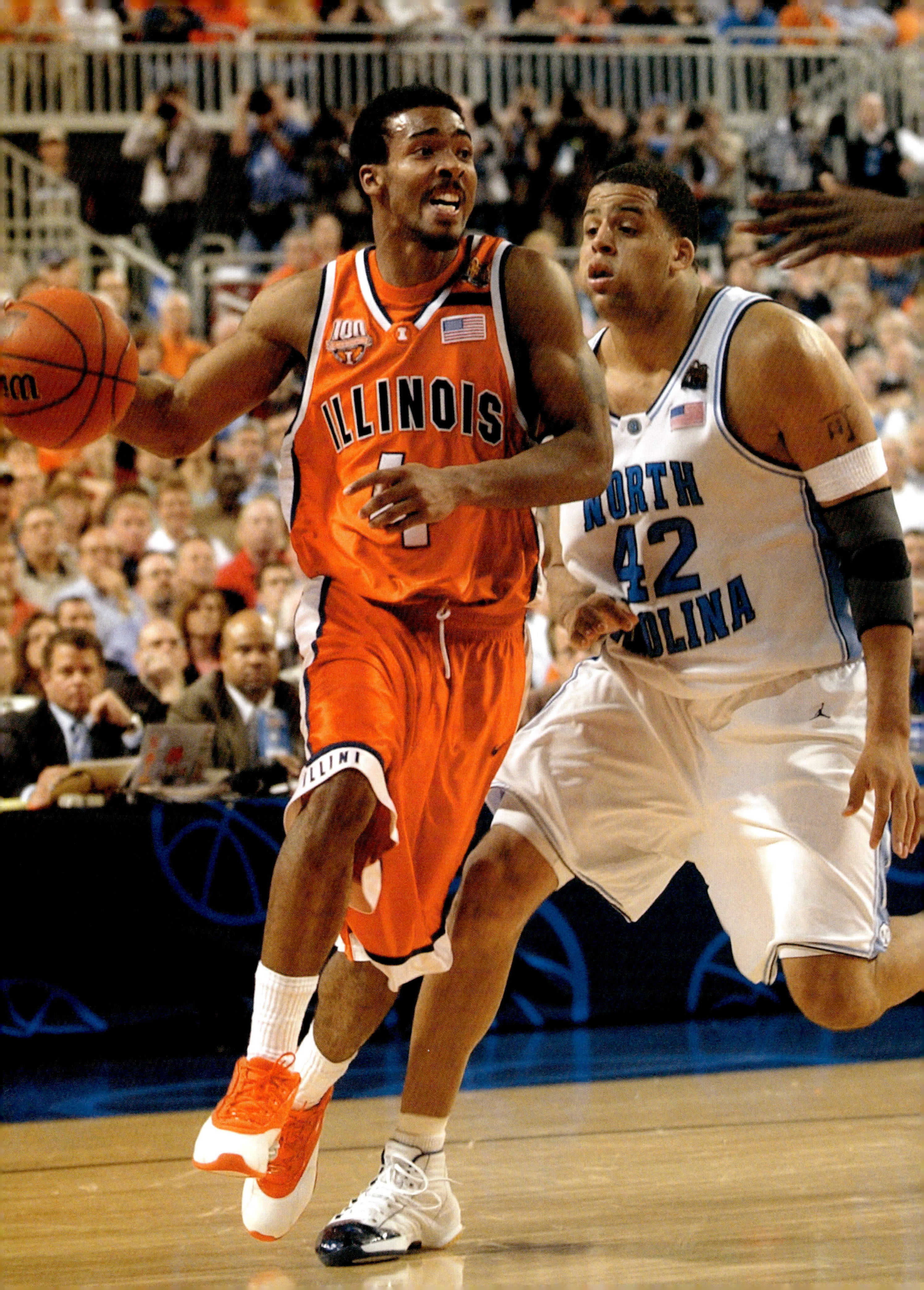
ILLINOIS
NORTH
42
ILLINI

all but buried early by a Carolina team that was bigger and stronger than the Illini and possessed the same cutthroat efficiency. The Tar Heels dominated the first half, jumping to a 40-27 lead by the break and leading by as many as 15 in the opening minutes of the second frame. But Illinois—as has been its custom—battled back.

"First half, they took the game to us," Brown said. "Second half, we came out and played Illinois basketball. We came out and fought 'em."

From 47-32 down, the Illini stormed to within two at 52-50. Then, after Tar Heels center Sean May scored seven straight points to put the Heels on top 65-55, the Illini roared back again, tying the game first at 65 and again at 70. And with the game still on the brink, Williams missed an open look from three-point range. Luther Head missed two.

"We made those shots all year," Williams said. "We just didn't have it tonight."

The Tar Heels had it. But just barely. Despite shooting 51.9 percent for the game and hitting 56.3 percent of their three-point tries, the Heels had to hang on against a team that shot 38.6 percent and went 12 of 40 from behind the three-point line—including one for its last 12.

"You cannot take anything away from those guys," said May, named the Final Four's Most Outstanding Player after scoring 26 points on 10-of-11 shooting. "They barreled back time and time again. Williams is a great player, and Brown is the heart of the team. Those guys never gave up. They are a hell of a team."

And Weber hopes you don't forget it.

"I hope the fans appreciate the journey," he said.

He hopes you're at Memorial Stadium at 5:30 on Tuesday evening to welcome his national runners-up back to Champaign. He hopes you scream and cheer and that for years to come you talk about his never-say-die Illini.

"I told them not to hang their heads," Weber said. "I told them they have nothing to be ashamed of, that they should be proud of everything they accomplished. We got beat by a great team. Where's the shame in that?"

The Illini lost a game but not their perspective.

"Nothing can change how we feel about this season," Brown said. "We were a team, a family, a bunch of guys that were humble and fought and never gave up. That's how I'm always going to remember this: just a great team and a great group of guys."

That group of guys was a shot here, a stop there from capping a near-perfect season with a perfect ending. But asked about the pain of coming so close, Weber broke out that smile of his again.

"I still love it. I still love the season. I love everything that happened. If we would've played the second half the way we played the first half, then I would've been disappointed."

When they shut down the Illinois locker room and players started to drift out, Williams stayed put. There were no tears, just a faraway gaze from a kid who might've played his last game in orange and blue. If it was, Williams will look back at it without regret. He could wonder forever what might've been. But he won't.

"It leaves a bad taste in your mouth right now, to lose and not get to cut down the nets," Williams had said a few minutes before. "But if you played your hearts out, you can't let it get you down. That's one thing we could say all year. We played our hearts out."

RIGHT: **Deron Williams played well in what many suspect will be his final college game, scoring 17 points, collecting seven assists and committing just one turnover.** *Elsa/Getty Images*

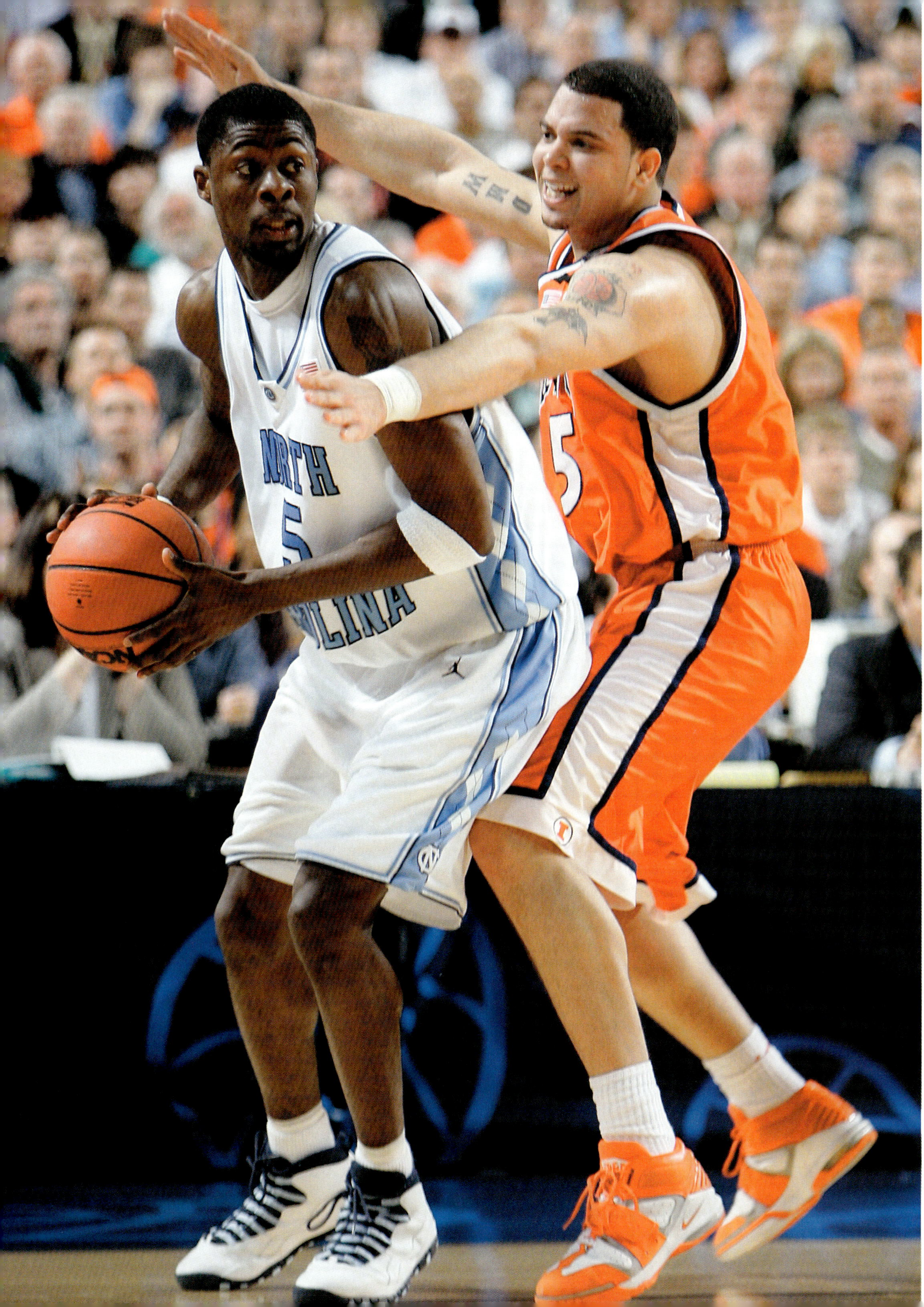
NORTH

ABOVE: Wherever the Illini went this season—from the Assembly Hall to the Arch of St. Louis—a sea of orange was sure to follow. *Doug Benc/Getty Images*

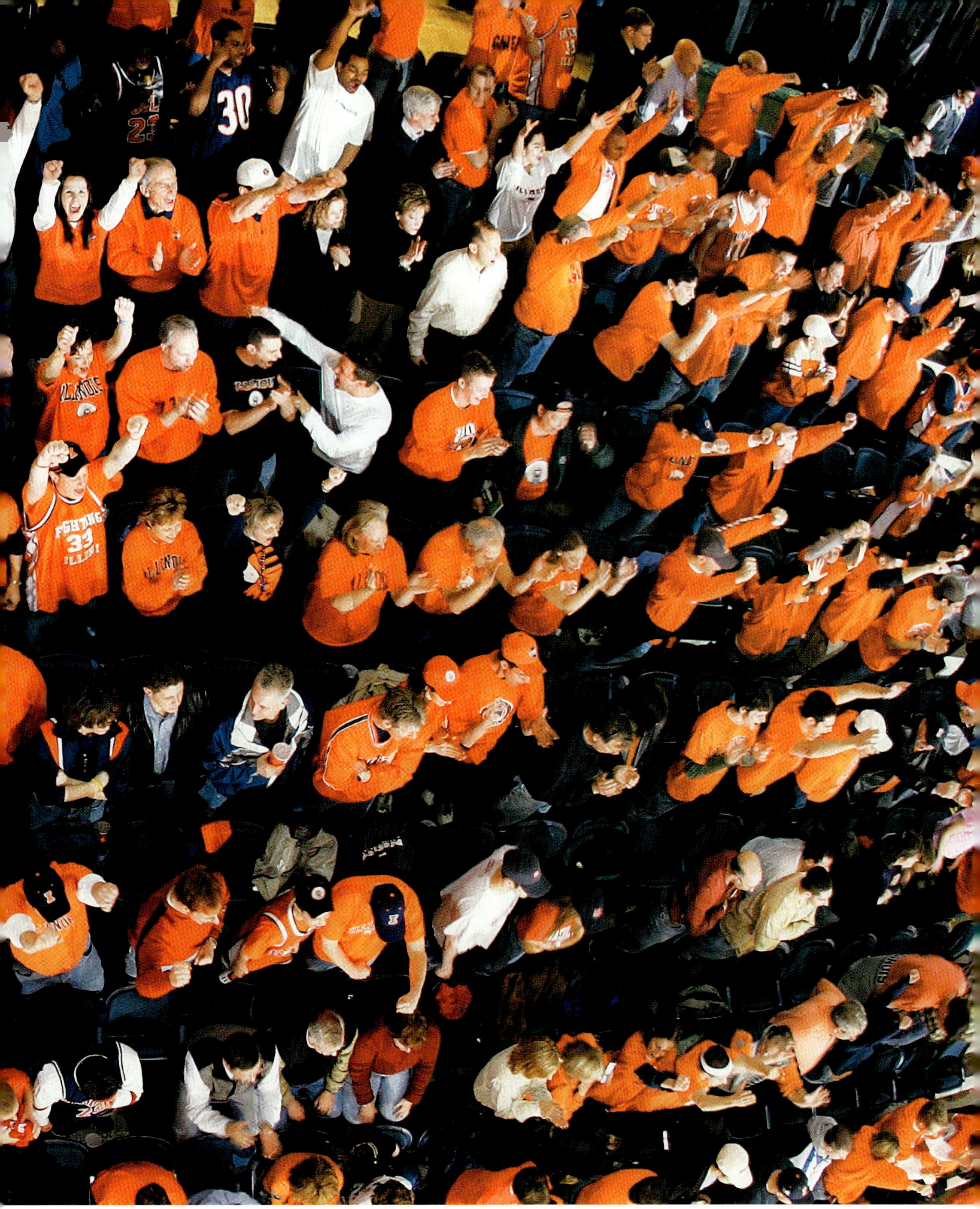
30
FIGHTING
33
ILLINI

2004-05 Season Statistics

PLAYER	GM	MIN	FG%	3FG%	FT%	REB	AST	TO	BLK	STL	TP
Head	39	33.3	46.3	41.0	78.8	4.0	3.8	1.8	0.2	1.7	16.0
Brown	39	32.6	49.9	43.4	77.2	2.7	4.5	1.9	0.1	1.8	13.3
Williams	39	33.7	43.3	36.4	67.7	3.6	6.8	2.8	0.2	1.0	12.5
Powell Jr.	39	25.1	54.9	38.5	72.9	5.7	0.4	1.1	0.2	0.6	12.0
Augustine	39	26.6	62.1	00.0	74.8	7.6	1.1	1.2	1.2	0.9	10.1
Ingram	39	15.1	47.3	39.1	79.3	2.7	0.4	0.4	0.5	0.7	4.5
Smith	38	10.9	40.6	36.4	65.2	2.1	0.6	0.6	0.5	0.3	3.3
McBride	38	14.4	32.3	31.0	1.000	1.3	0.8	0.5	0.1	0.4	2.6
Carter	33	7.9	51.6	16.7	47.4	1.8	0.2	0.4	0.2	0.3	2.2
Pruitt	21	4.6	38.5	00.0	50.0	0.9	0.0	0.5	0.1	0.1	1.4
Nkemdi	18	2.4	60.0	00.0	00.0	0.3	0.1	0.3	0.1	0.0	0.7
Totals	**39**	—	**48.4**	**39.2**	**72.8**	**34.3**	**18.6**	**11.0**	**3.2**	**7.7**	**77.0**
Opponents	39	—	41.5	35.8	66.5	31.3	12.4	14.9	2.5	5.0	61.1

Season Results

Date	Opponent	Location	Result	Leading Scorer
11/19/2004	Delaware State	Assembly Hall	W, 87-67	Brown, 17
11/21/2004	Florida A&M	Assembly Hall	W, 91-60	Brown, 20
11/24/2004	Oakland	Assembly Hall	W, 85-54	Head, 22
11/27/2004	Gonzaga	Conseco Fieldhouse	W, 89-72	Williams/Head, 20
12/01/2004	Wake Forest	Assembly Hall	W, 91-73	Powell Jr., 19
12/04/2004	Arkansas	Alltel Arena	W, 72-60	Powell Jr., 19
12/06/2004	Chicago State	Assembly Hall	W, 78-59	Head, 17
12/09/2004	Georgetown	MCI Center	W, 74-59	Powell Jr., 19
12/11/2004	Oregon	United Center	W, 83-66	Head, 23
12/19/2004	Valparaiso	Assembly Hall	W, 93-56	Brown, 19
12/22/2004	Missouri	Savvis Center	W, 70-64	Head, 20
12/27/2004	Longwood	Assembly Hall	W, 105-79	Williams, 23
12/30/2004	Northwestern State	Valley High School	W, 69-51	Head, 18
12/31/2004	Cincinnati	Valley High School	W, 67-45	Williams, 18
01/05/2005	Ohio State	Assembly Hall	W, 84-65	Augustine, 21
01/08/2005	Purdue	Mackey Arena	W, 68-59	Head, 15
01/12/2005	Penn State	Assembly Hall	W, 90-64	Head, 19
01/15/2005	Northwestern	Welsh-Ryan Arena	W, 78-66	Head, 26
01/20/2005	Iowa	Assembly Hall	W, 73-68	Head, 25
01/25/2005	Wisconsin	Kohl Center	W, 75-65	Head, 18
01/29/2005	Minnesota	Assembly Hall	W, 89-66	Powell Jr., 21
02/01/2005	Michigan State	Breslin Center	W, 81-68	Head, 22
02/06/2005	Indiana	Assembly Hall	W, 60-47	Augustine, 16
02/08/2005	Michigan	Crisler Arena	W, 57-51	Brown, 16
02/12/2005	Wisconsin	Assembly Hall	W, 70-59	Head, 26
02/16/2005	Penn State	Bryce Jordan Center	W, 83-63	Powell Jr., 21
02/19/2005	Iowa	Carver-Hawkeye Arena	W, 75-65	Williams/Brown, 18
02/23/2005	Northwestern	Assembly Hall	W, 84-48	Brown, 20
03/03/2005	Purdue	Assembly Hall	W, 84-50	Brown, 27
03/06/2005	Ohio State	Value City Arena	L, 65-64	Brown, 13

Big Ten Tournament

Date	Opponent	Location	Result	Leading Scorer
03/11/2005	Northwestern	United Center	W, 68-51	Augustine, 15
03/12/2005	Minnesota	United Center	W, 64-56	Head, 14
03/13/2005	Wisconsin	United Center	W, 54-43	Powell Jr., 15

NCAA Tournament

Date	Opponent	Location	Result	Leading Scorer
03/17/2005	Fairleigh Dickinson	RCA Dome	W, 67-55	Brown, 19
03/19/2005	Nevada	RCA Dome	W, 71-59	Augustine, 23
03/24/2005	Wisconsin-Milwaukee	Allstate Arena	W, 77-63	Williams/Brown, 21
03/26/2005	Arizona	Allstate Arena	W, 90-89	Williams, 22
04/02/2005	Louisville	Edward Jones Dome	W, 72-57	Head/Powell Jr., 20
04/04/2005	North Carolina	Edward Jones Dome	L, 75-70	Head, 21

CONGRATULATIONS ILLINOIS!

Dean's Architectural and Specialized Reprographics
404 E. University Ave. • www.deansblueprint.com • 217-359-3261
Since 1964

CHAMPAIGN • ILLINOIS

UNFORGETTABLE

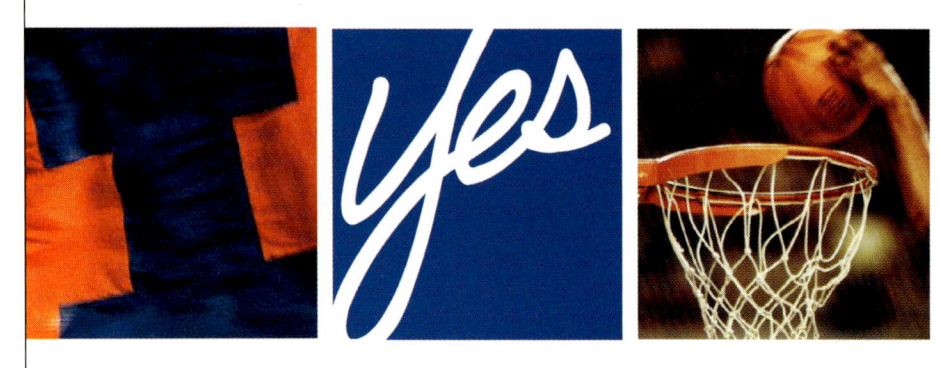

Serving Illini fans from
eleven central Illinois locations

Champaign - Decatur - Effingham - Springfield
800.872.0081 www.hickorypointbank.com

HICKORY POINT BANK & TRUST, fsb

Member FDIC

Thanks for a memorable season!

Busey

Congratulations Fighting Illini Coaches and Players

Busey Bank*
First Busey Trust & Investment Co.
First Busey Securities, Inc.**

Serving Champaign, Ford, McLean, Peoria, and Tazewell Counties

*Member FDIC   www.busey.com   **Member NASD/SIPC

Tom Cain & Company

RE/MAX REALTY ASSOCIATES

PHONE: 217-352-5700
TOM@SOLTEC.NET
www.CAINandCOMPANY.com

EACH OFFICE INDEPENDENTLY OWNED AND OPERATED

OUR TEAM SUPPORTS YOUR TEAM! GO ILLINI!! CONGRATULATIONS AND THANK YOU FOR AN EXCITING AND MEMORABLE YEAR!

Hendrick House

Now Celebrating more than 58 years in Student Housing

- Carpeted Rooms
- Semi Private Baths
- Completely Air Conditioned
- Weekly Maid Service
- Highly Acclaimed Meals
- Free Tutoring

THE ONLY PRIVATELY OWNED RESIDENCE HALL NEAR:
ENGINEERING CAMPUS
COMPUTER SCIENCE
BECKMAN INSTITUTE

Green & Lincoln, Urbana, IL 61801
(217) 365-8000 • (217) 356-3344
http://www.hendrickhouse.com

Freshmen Approved Housing!

CONGRATULATIONS ILLINI

Rental City

When you need it now—but not eternally—JUST RENT IT!

2508 N. MATTIS AVE. | 217-359-6127

McLane Midwest

DON'T LET YOUR CAREER HANG ON THE RIM.

Come join the winning Driving team at McLane Midwest Danville, IL!

Interested CDL Drivers contact:
1-800-851-8490
Hiring for Illinois and Kentucky

Go ILLINI!

SP116254

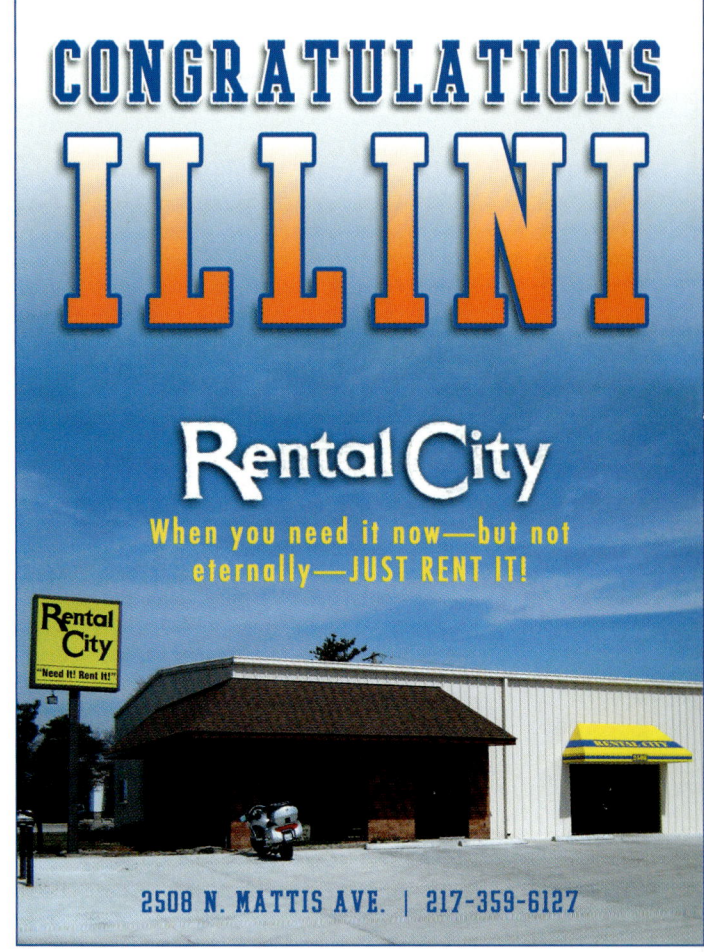

Celebrating 50 Years!

BIRKEY'S
Fifty Years 1954-2004

Serving You With These Quality Brands

CASE IH · eXmark · CASE
Kubota · JACOBSEN

BIRKEY'S LOCATIONS	Gibson City, IL (217) 784-4281	Hudson, IL (309) 726-1132
Urbana, IL - AG (217) 337-1772	Hoopeston, IL (217) 283-5191	Mattoon, IL - CE (217) 235-3158
Urbana, IL - CE (217) 337-1781	Macomb, IL (309) 837-1700	Attica, IN - Auto (765) 764-1637
Oakland, IL (217) 346-2312	Galesburg, IL (309) 341-4360	Williamsport, IN (765) 762-6153

SUCCESS IS BUILT ONE BLOCK AT A TIME. CONGRATULATIONS TO THE FIGHTING ILLINI MEN'S BASKETBALL TEAM ON A TERRIFIC 2004-2005 SEASON.

The Atkins Group

Community. Team. Dedication.

Congratulations to the Fighting Illini Men's Basketball Team. You've captured our hearts during this historic and unforgettable journey. You deserve nothing less than a standing ovation.

bank for community. bank for life.

17 branches located throughout Central Illinois

EQUAL HOUSING LENDER. MEMBER FDIC.   www.centralillinoisbank.com   CIB Central Illinois Bank

---

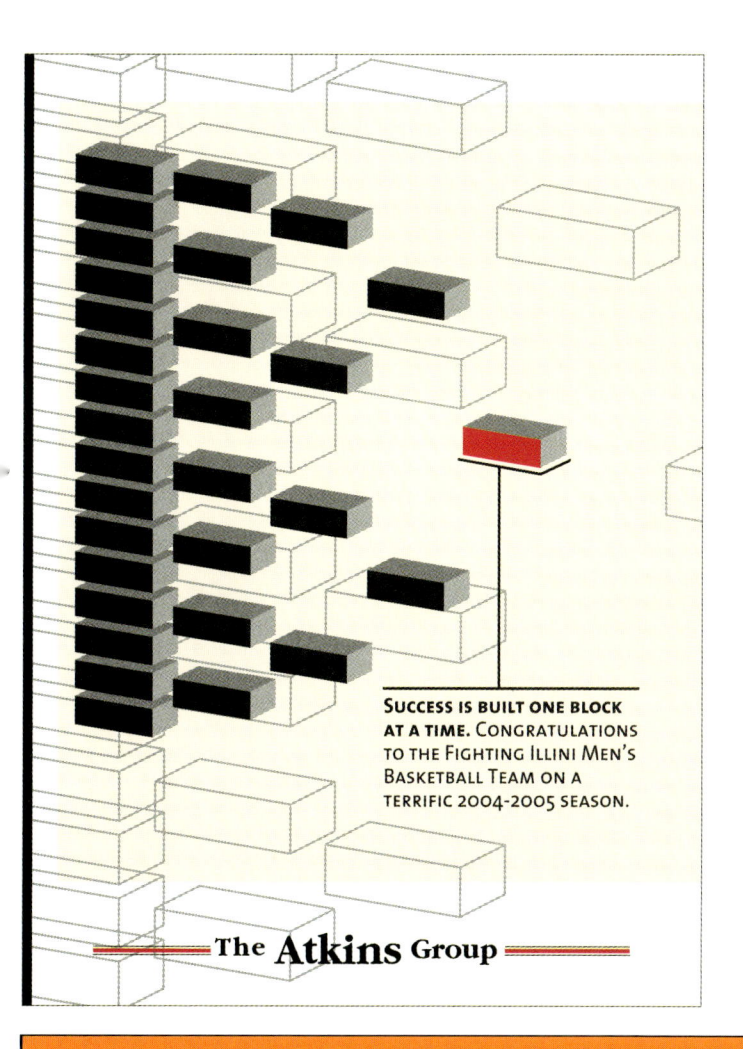

Sports Publishing — The Official Publisher for the American Sports Fan — Congratulates the Illinois Fighting Illini on an Incredible 2004-05 Season!

Celebrate the Illini's Final Four Appearance with a Variety of Other Illinois Sports Titles.

Available Now at:
www.SportsPublishingLLC.com

SP SPORTS PUBLISHING L.L.C.

Orders may also be placed 24-hours-a-day at 217-363-2072 or toll-free,
1-877-424-BOOK (2665)

Go Illini!

Acknowledgments

The entire staff of *The News-Gazette* contributed to the coverage of the 2004-05 Illinois men's basketball season.

We gratefully acknowledge the efforts of the sports and photography departments:

Sports Department

Sports editor: Jim Rossow

Illinois men's basketball beat writer: Brett Dawson

Columnist: Loren Tate

Staff writers: Bob Asmussen, Tony Bleill, Brian Dietz, Jeff Huth, Fred Kroner, Jeff Mezydlo.

Copy editors: Rich Barak, Mike Goebel, Tony Mancuso

Photography Department

Photo editor: Darrell Hoemann

Photographers: Vanda Bidwell, Heather Coit, Rick Danzl, John Dixon, Holly Hart, Robert K. O'Daniell, Robin Scholz

Photo lab technician: Dan Wendt